TOTAL TELEMARKING

BRAD ENGLISH

East River Publishing Company
Crested Butte, Colorado

Photo Credits:

Front cover: Doug Buzzell/
photo by Steve Buzzell

Page 6 by Jack Marcial
Back Cover by Greg Dalbey

**Library of Congress Catalog Card Number:
83-83417**

English, Bradley N., 1952-

Total Telemarking

ISBN 0-915789-00-0
East River Publishing Company, Box 654,
Crested Butte, Colorado, 81224

Copyright © 1984 by Brad English.
All rights reserved.

Printed in the United States by
Crested Butte Printing, Co.

DEDICATION

To the Ski to Die Club

whose members teach by doing,

and to my parents,

who somehow understand my

Sisyphean fanaticism for

going up and down mountains,

This book is gratefully dedicated.

Fortune Favors the Brave:

Live to ski,

Ski to die

And live to ski another day.

CONTRIBUTORS

I. Writers

Dr. Duane Vandenbusche
Eric Burr
Ned Gillette
Tom Carr
Peter Dea
Keith Calhoun
Dale Gallagher

Bob Jamieson
Denis Hall
Paul Parker
Wayne Hanson
Chris Noble
David Blehert

II. Photographers/Artists

Nathan Bilow
Jim Kahnweiler
Mike Carr
Peter Dea
Eric Burr
Eric Sanford
Doug Pierson

Greg Dalbey
Jack Marcial
Rick Borkovec
Paul Gallaher
Craig Hall
Steve Buzzell
Katie Marshall

III. Technical Assistance

Eric Sanford
Don Portman
Rick Borkovec
Steve Barnett
Todd Azud

ACKNOWLEDGMENTS

Special thanks are also due to many other people, without whose patience and support this dream-book would not have been possible. They include:

- Beth McCurry, for turning hundreds of pages of handwritten copy into a typed, finished manuscript;
- Katie Marshall, for assignment work in Sweden and Norway;
- Pat Crow, of The Ideaworks Ad Agency, for her invaluable advice and cover design;
- Jeannine McMurry, for fast and accurate typesetting;
- Susan Sparks, for layout and paste-up;
- Steve Glazer, for everything;
- Vern Stupple, for editing of Chapter II, *The Dawn of Ski;*
- Dave Moe, of *Powder Magazine;*
- The staff at Crested Butte Printing;
- The Phoenix Ski Corp., Aspen, Co.;
- Crested Butte Mountain Resort, and the townspeople of Crested Butte, Co.

Helicopter powder guides Jack Marcial and Craig Hall in the backcountry.

CONTENTS

I	Introduction	10
II	The Dawn of Ski/A History	13
III	Telemark Turning Today: The Fun-damentals	35
IV	Special Conditions/Advanced Technique	51
V	Telemark Racing	71
VI	Nordic Ski-Mountaineering: The Creme de la Creme	81
VII	Expeditions to the Ultimate: Extreme Cross-Country	103

The author in Glacier National Park, Montana/ Greg Dalbey Photo

I lift my eyes from the incredibly inclined horizon to the dazzling cerulean sky above. It is breathless, yet vibrant and alive. Frost hangs suspended in the early morning air, like crystal droplets shimmering; the snow is a mirror of dancing reflections.

First light warms my right shoulder and slashes a golden ribbon across the summit ridge to my left. Below, the valley remains shrouded in green-black-blueness. The very top, drenched in sun, and its northern headwall, exist only in my imagination.

Reality right now is the irridescent snow beneath my skis, the switch-backs remaining to the saddle above, and my four companions coming up the track below.

The snow seems stable on this southeastern side, with no signs of settling or sluffing. It's been forty-eight cold hours since the last storm spread 2½-feet on the upper slopes, and expectations are high for perfect powder skiing. Still, my pulse if fast, and the sound of my heart in my ears is louder than the electronic "peep--peep" of the rescue device on my chest. I hasten to put on my wind parka and shoulder my pack again.

I make my last few steps to the saddle slowly and deliberately though...my line of traverse is vertically extended to the maximum. My weight shifts as evenly as it can on such a radically inclined field of deep powder, my body canted forward, boots flexing and heels free. The summit stands close by up a corniced ridge-ramp; I am at thirteen thousand-feet and going higher.

Suddenly I peak out on the summit, and a whole new reality opens up before me. Once climbed, the mountain reveals -- like a curtain drawn back on the portals of perception -- what it has hidden. Time and Space stretch out further than consciousness can grasp; the here and now of being on this summit is overwhelming. Beyond all my hopes and fears, the peaks go on and on...the rivers flow in all directions. The living land lies bathed in the glory of a new day, and the cosmos sings all around.

The great northern headwall, draped in aquamarine, drops away beneath me and pours itself into lower bowls. Like the alabaster form of a reclining lover, the snow rolls and beckons its essential invitation. My companions come up one by one and stand in silent awe as I, knowing the best is yet to come.

A snow pit is dug, a brief but serious consultation is held, and we're throwing on our powder suits as heads nod in agreement...eyes bugging out behind tinted goggles, grinning like fools. Motivation at maximum, perception at peak, we're in full throttle. All systems are "Go!" and the field is clear for take-off.

The first skier over the edge carves a hesitant traverse -- cautious and concise -- as the rest watch on in focused anticipation.

He crosses quickly to a zone of safety, kick turns to face toward the chute again, and waits. Nothing happens. He traverses halfway out the snowfield once more, pauses, and then turns his skis loose down the fall line. He looks back once, and then disappears in a cloud of powder.

Then it's everyone for himself, kids: if you snooze, you lose. But of course we couldn't ski it all even if we climbed back up until moonlight, and so we each experience our own untracked lines.

Encapsuled in powder, suspended in bottomless snow, approaching weightlessness, 'Warp Nine,' and the Time/Space Continuum, I flow downhill for 3,000 vertical-feet. Being and doing are finally fused, forming the totality of existence.

We keep an eye on one another (because my beeper's no good without your beeper, buddy),

First tracks powder: Five Zen lines/ J. Marcial Photo

and it's all happening just right. We barely break stride until we hit the river bottom.

Then, leaning on poles and panting like race horses, we turn to look at our artwork. Five precise strokes stream from the slash of sky, snake down the headwall and dart through the bowls. They are the individual expressions of a joy in Creation...the visible traces of the Dance of Life. They will be gone tomorrow from the face of the earth, yet they will live on in our spirits forever.

With one last look over our shoulders, we begin the homeward ski.

1 INTRODUCTION

From its ancient beginnings to its current popularity, cross-country skiing has continued to develop as a rich and broad experience. In work, sport and art, the nordic ski is both tool and toy. It provides the fulfillment of physical exercise, the ease of winter travel, the accessibility of snow-covered summits and steep, swooping slopes; the Zen of the flow and a knowledge of self.

Cross-country skiing's many forms are practiced by millions of people around the world, on diverse levels and for different reasons. One of its ultra expressions, ski-mountaineering --or trekking on skis to high peaks in order to descend their snowfields on the same equipment -- incorporates all aspects of the art. An overland approach, ski ascent, wilderness routefinding, snow science, weather wisdom, emergency medical aid, winter survival and mountain experience are as essential to the downhill run as that first turn off the top.

Telemark skiing is only a part of this whole cross-country adventure, but an important and practical one nonetheless. It fuses the basic elements of several techniques with unique versatility, effective on flat ground or slope, in touring, racing or jumping.

Although virtually ignored until recently, the ancient principles of the telemark turn have been rediscovered and refined, opening up whole new realms of possibility. Thus, after centuries of limited development, cross country technology and techniques are only now beginning to realize their full potential.

Each skier has his or her own definition of enjoyment, method of approach and sense of style, and each is equally valid. At the same time, whether nordic or alpine, telemark or parallel, ski-area or backcountry, downhill or cross-country, each ski style has its own strengths and weaknesses, each approach its own limitations and potential.

Thousands of books have been written on the sport of skiing, including hundreds about the cross-country approach. Some have touched on nordic downhill skills but few -- if any -- have ever thoroughly covered skiing's oldest turn: the telemark. If only for this reason, it deserves further study.

In this book I've tried to provide as comprehensive a guide as possible to the myriad modes of telemark skiing --its origins and ap-

Telemark and parallel tracks in Wasatch powder/ *Kerry Walton* photo

plications, its fundamentals and state of the art from past to present.

The following advice comes from experts all, most of whom I have studied with over the past ten years. Included are the very pioneers directly responsible for telemark turning's current renaissance, plus some of the fastest racers on the pro slalom circuit today, certified instructors, helicopter powder guides, expedition leaders, and search and rescue personnel. I think you'll find their individual approaches and unique perspectives offer valuable insights on every level, whether you're an advanced or beginner, nordic or alpine skier.

Of course, there are countless other experts I've not mentioned, who are constantly pushing the limits of the known in all situations. No book can remain completely current.

Also, no book can offer as much instruction as one's own experience and experimentation on snow and skis. And nothing can hinder your improvement in, or appreciation of an activity like, 'too much technique.'

Above all, there is no final form in skiing -- past, present or future. It is instead an on-going art, a process: open to new interpretation, yet fundamentally natural and enjoyable.

Brad English

Brad English
Crested Butte, Colorado
1984

The first known record of skiing, carved on a Norwegian cave wall between 2,500-5,000 B.C.

The wandering tribes of the past have found their homes and have settled down. But their descendants have inherited something of the spirit which urged them toward new expanses of snow, and something of their unconquerable desire to master the winged boards.

If this be fanaticism, let us make the most of it. For there are few forms of human exuberance more conducive to good health, good will, and good sport.

Charles M. Dudley

II THE DAWN OF SKI/A HISTORY

*We shall not cease from exploration
And the end of all our exploring
Will be to arrive where we started
And know the place for the first time*

T.S. Eliot

Skiing's first tracks were carved across the glacial ice of man-the-toolmaker's early existence, in a time and place beyond the scope of recorded history. Although its exact origins are uncertain, and its most ancient techniques unknown, the art of striding on skis helped open the way for the evolution of human culture in the four corners of the world, and has been consistently utilized for at least seven millenia.

The mobility of ski running, or "the white art,"[1] provided primitive man the means of hunting for daily survival in a harsh and limited environment. With the ski (fr. Old Norse skith, skei to cut, split of wood)[2], tribes were able to migrate more freely, thereby increasing communication and trade among diverse peoples, and uniting scattered settlements as interdependent communities. It helped defend nations against invasion during times of war, and saved lives in times of peace.

Throughout the centuries, the technology of skiing's tools and the intricacies of its techniques have undergone considerable refinement, particularly in the last one hundred years. Yet the basic system discovered long ago still holds true today, and remains the most efficient means of self locomotion over snow ever devised.

The telemark turn, for example, considered to be a relatively modern technique developed by Sondre Norheim of Telemark, Norway in the mid-1800's, led to a rapid development of skiing's methodology, material and style. In many ways, though, the history of the telemark approach parallels the history of the ski, and there are signs that its roots may be almost as ancient.

At the same time, "the popularity of the revitalized telemarking style -- having come full circle -- marks the end of an era of overspecialization, and for many skiers...is ultimately the most useful and versatile form of skiing around."[3]

After all, the basic telemark stance -- the foundation for the more complex turn -- is both a natural extension of the cross-country diagonal stride, and the most stable position

"A steep descent"/from A.B. Block, 1889

The Ovrebo Ski relic

possible in changing conditions. Likewise, the telemark turn remains one of the most efficient means of controlled descent on free-heeled bindings and flexible boots ever devised.

Of the various types of ski which have been classified, the telemark model is one of the earliest and most important of the main designs. Above all, it was meant to turn.

The Historiska Museet in Stockholm, Sweden, contains the Hoting Ski, "pronounced the oldest known to the world."[4] Found in the peat bogs at Angermanland, this fragment is believed to be between 4,000 and 5,000 years old. Sledge runners dating back to 7,000 B.C., however, suggest the ski may have been used much earlier.[5]

Norweg. Sprung-Ski (Typus Telemark)
Länge 2,30 m, Breite 7,5 cm, Gewicht 2,3 - 2,5 Kg

Telemark skis of the 1800's

TOOLS FOR THE TELEMARKER

Skis

The classic telemark turn is a uniquely nordic technique, based on the arcing nature of two moving skis angled together to form a single dynamic curve. When properly weighted and emphatically steered, even barrel staves or 2" x 4'''s can be made to turn. Obviously, the better the equipment the more effective the technique.

While the basic principles discovered long ago still hold true today -- no matter how crude your boards -- modern ski technology is rapidly transforming the natue of advanced technique. Thus, after centuries of limited development, the nordic approach is only now beginning to realize its full potential.

The more 'alpine' in design and materials cross-country downhill skis become, the closer to a parallel turn the telemark can become, since each ski's sidecut is capable of carving an arc independent of the other. As a result, either method (or any method!) of turning on nordic gear is more effective than ever before. Basically, if you want to turn, I recommend you choose a ski that's meant to turn!

For example, the Phoenix Ski Company, of Aspen, Co., manufactures two of the best all around cross-country downhill skis ever designed.

The Wilderness Series

This ski is a wet-wrap fiber glass torsion box ski, with a foam core. It has an urethane sidewall and an aluminum tail protector, coupled with full-length cracked steel edges to give it more flexibility. It is a double cambered ski. And while it will ski hardpack better than most, it is particularly well suited for backcountry travel and powder skiing. The Phoenix Mountain Edge Wilderness Series is a very good all around ski.

The Racing Series

This ski is also wet-wrap glass torsion box construction with a foam core. The Racing Series has urethane sidewalls, aluminum, tail protector and a full length continuous steel edge. This ski is single cambered to give the best possible hold on hardpack and ice.

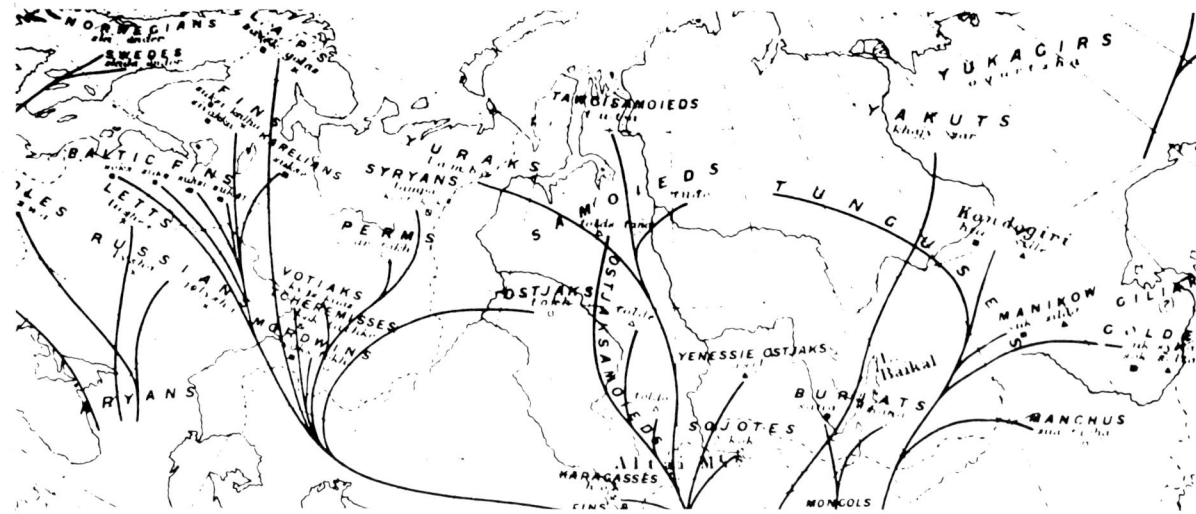

Distribution of ancient skis and the various names by which they were known, according to C. Dudley

While the Hoting Ski is more of a snowshoe-shaped board in design, the 2,500 year old Ovrebo Ski, from southern Norway, has a curved and pointed tip, "...quite like the Telemark Model (of the 1800's) in its grace...It has the same bend and...bearing surface...tapered in at the middle with the same slight flare at the tail."[6]

Those skis discovered in the Altais Range of Central Asia, near Lake Baykhal where Mongolia meets the Great Gobi Desert to the south, are currently dated to have been made around 2,500 B.C., "...and they bear a startling resemblance to those in use today."[7]

One theory, put forward by Charles M. Dudley in 1935, maintains the ski was originated in this region of China and carried westward to Europe by migrating tribes.

Citing numerous errors in Dudley's supporting data, modern historians (most notably, Ted Bays), disagree with Dudley, and argue that the ski was born in Scandanavia. Yet, I wonder...

Coming from the Pamirs, the Aryans, forerunners of the Caucasian race, did indeed cross the Caucasus, Carpathian and Alpine Ranges to settle Germany and the Scandanavian Peninsula; while the parents of the Finns, Lapps and Hungarians crossed the Great Kirghiz Steppes to settle Russia, Sweden, Norway, Finland and Hungary.

Likewise, the Samoids (a tribe of Eskimo), the Turks, Mongols and Tunguses scattered throughout Siberia,[8] while the Eskimo reached the North American Arctic "...from Asia across the Bering Strait, or a then existing land bridge, or even the ice farther north, not earlier than 20,000 years ago."[9]

Could these primitive tribes actually have crossed such massive mountain barriers, or the immense expanses of frozen plains which lay between, without some form of ski? As Dudley writes:

> It is reasonable to believe that the peoples who migrated from the various parts of the Altai Mountains carried...the ski with them and put them to use in their new homes. Many of the short wide ski which have been uncovered in various parts of Europe and Asia are quite like the snowshoe board.
> This, plus the fact that all the names which have been applied to the boards fall into one of four linguistic groups, is...evidence that ski were of common origin and that common origin was the Altai Mtns. of Central Asia.[10]

It also seems possible that China's relatively unexplored regions could contain ski relics, as yet undiscovered, which outdate any of those found in Scandanavia. If so, the future may yet prove Dudley correct.

Whether or not the ski did emerge from the Far East, we know they were certainly used by tribes of Northmen in the late and postglacial stages of North European inhabitation, from the North Sea to northern Japan.[11]

Regardless of who actually invented the ski, we can't help but marvel at the magnitude of their achievement. What inspired such a design, unlike anything that exists in nature? What did others think as they witnessed the birth of the ski, centuries before the first known record of the wheel?[12]

Truger: predecessor of the ski?

Did they chuckle in their beards, those old, wise ones, and say it would never work? Did they watch in silence, wondering, as a craftsman's hands shaped matter to the unique image in his mind? When, with tools of stone he or she fashioned the original skis and carried them out to the snow, did the others yet understand? When he hit powder snow, did he telemark?

While no record exists to answer these questions, the ancestors of that first skier have passed on a considerable amount of information to help future generations master the winged boards.

Through art and artifacts, folklore, religion and literature, peoples around the world have proudly depicted their sport for posterity: accounts of a way of life on skis.

Ancient caving drawings, such as those found in Norway and Russia, suggest the development of skiing was a matter of survival above all else.

17th century woodcarving

Bison, reindeer, grizzly bear, elk, wolves, sea lion, sheep and smaller prey provided the food, shelter, clothing and utensils of primitive man's very existence. As tribal hunters pursued these herds of game in their cyclical migrations along the receeding edges of glacial ice, the ski was an invaluable tool.

With the aid of the ski, it became much easier to hunt the swifter animals in winter, when deep snow slowed their progress and sped the pursuing hunter.[13] Unfortunately, it has been theorized that the lack of elk in the Scandanavian Peninsula today is a direct result of the skill of these old ski hunters.[14]

> They make boards out of wood, which they call "sana" or "hana" (fr. ON striding on ski), they fasten them on their feet with straps, take a staff in their hand and press this staff against the earth, so...they glide...on the snow.
> So they hunt over the Steppes and level country, as if they were riding on elks...The booty of their hunt they lay on another sled which they draw after them...
> Whoever understands how to run can go quickly forward.[15]

Olaus Magnus, the Archbishop of Upsala, wrote a book in 1555 A.D., that introduced Norwegian skiing to Europe. Published in Italy, it is full of pictures of hunting on skis, and tales of skiers betting on their individual speed and prowess.[16]

Imagine yourself in their place, stalking on skis the elusive quarry which may feed many families. It is cold dawn, 1000 B.C.

You are gliding through a snowy wood, dipping down gullies, swift and silent. Sensing game ahead, you drop quickly onto one knee, croached low behind a tree blind. You remain poised yet motionless, breathlessly alert, with your bow arm across your forward knee.

After a moment, you stride from your cover, sail across the dark edge of the meadow and over a knoll. As you hit the bottom of the drop, you might very well kneel down low again over your skis, with one foot forward and knee up, the other foot back and knee just above the ground. Both legs are spread wide for lateral stability and flexed to absorb the shock

Birkebeiner Vikings with the infant Prince of Norway.

of your sudden compression.

When descending another slope, you might use this same stance to pivot your skis quickly to a halt, or swerve around trees without stopping. The first time this was actually done, the technique we know today as the telemark turn was born.

With the mastery of ski running -- or "the white art"[17] -- man began to transcend the barriers of his harsh and limited environment.

Gradually, the expertise of such folk as the Skriddfinnar (or "gliding Finns" described by Procopius in 526 A.D.[18]), spread from land to land. As the old Norwegian verse goes:

> There are three lines running through Norwegian history.
> One is the furrow scored by the peasant's plowshare.
> The second, the wake of the Norwegian ship across the seven seas.
> The third, the ski tracks that girdle the Earth.[19]

According to the Sagas of Snorre, written in 900 A.D., the Vikings were, "excellent skiers." For them, skiing was a sacred part of religion as well as a means of day-to-day survival. They worshipped such dieties as Uller, the god of winter who was pictured on skis, and Skada, also known as Odurrdid, the goddess of ski.

The old Norse Myth of the founding of Norway relates how the god Nor, considered the father of all Norwegians, used skis to overcome the drifts of a great snow blizzard and continue on to forge a nation.

Like the gods they worshipped, the feats of these Norwegian 'wonder skiers' became almost legendary in their magnitude. Rightfully proud of their heritage, Norwegians still reenact an event that occurred in 1206.

After years of civil war, with King Sverre dead and his faithful followers forced to live as outlaws marked by birch-covered ski boots, all hope of a unified Norway rested with two year-old Prince Haakon Haakonson.

When the enemy threatened to seize this rightful heir, two members of the Birkebeiner Viking Tribe ("Birch-legs"), carried the infant prince to safety by skiing 55 km. (or roughly 31-miles), over the snow-covered mountains between Lillenhammer and Rena. The rescued Haakon became King, and the nation was reunited. Today, Norway commemorates this event in the Birkebeiner Citizen's Nordic Race over the same route, which has drawn thousands of competitors each year since 1932.[20]

In a parallel adventure of national dimensions, the ski can be said to have saved Sweden when the Danes led, "the bloodbath of Stockholm."[21] Gustav Erickson Vasa, the massacre's sole surviving Swedish nobleman, had fled to the mountainous borders. To bring back this leader and drive out the invaders, two Swedish skiers strode from Mora over 90 km., searched for and found him. When they returned, Sweden was restored, and since 1922 the Gustav Vasa Loppett Series cross-country competition has celebrated this feat.

Even though modern-day Birkebeiner and Loppett racers don't use the telemark turn when they run their prepared track, Haakon's rescuers probably did. Avoiding roads and the possibility of detection, perhaps traveling at night, they carried a child as well as their weapons and other essential gear over every condition imaginable. Since falling was out of the question, the increased stability of the low, wide telemark stance might well have been a natural part of their survival-style skiing.

Whatever technique those Vikings used, turning skills have definitely been a part of all-around cross-country skiing for centuries. As Valvasor wrote in the 1500's: "There is no mountain so precipitous and so grown over with large trees that they cannot descend it in this fashion (on skis). For they wind and distort their descent like a snake."[22] In recognition, telemark slalom downhill racing was added to the 1982 United States counterpart of the Birkebeiner competition held in Telemark, Wisconsin.

In addition to hunting, travel, and search and rescue, the ski was used to deliver mail in Norway beginning in 1535. Accounts describe, "lonely farmers who are glad when they hear the distant sound of the post horn and the mailman arrives on skis with messages from relatives and friends."[23]

Skilled as such skiers must have been, the most important advancements in technique seem to have occurred during those times of violent conflict and competitive sport.

"On the level"/
A.B. Block

Ski-troopers of WW I

Norwegian ski-sport as depicted in 1881/Katie Marshall photo copy

The Ski Goes To War

The first formal corps of ski troopers was formed by Norway in 1718, and similar units have since played a vital role in many of history's greatest military engagements. Their effectiveness on the snowy fields of mortal combat was clearly proven when Lieutenant Jans Henrick Emmahusen, from Trondheim, Norway, led a 242-man ski patrol and overcame a superior Swedish stronghold during the twenty-year-long, Great North Wars.[24]

The same Lt. Emmahusen also wrote Norway's first ski manual in 1733[25], a book that was to revolutionize technique by introducing the use of skis of equal length. This new regulation was a radical departure from the standard Osterdal System, wherein a short ski was used as a 'kicker,' in conjunction with a longer, gliding ski.

Colonel Georges Bilgeri, who, with Mathius Zdarsky, taught the Austrian Kaiserjaeger Mtn. Troops to ski during WWI, introduced the use of two ski poles in 1915.[26]

Lowell Thomas describes his experiences with the Italian ski troops during December, 1917 -- when, as a journalist, he was taken to their *refugio* near the 13,000' summit of Monte Rosa on the Austrian frontier: "The *Arditi* were nerveless young men who climbed cliffs with knives in their teeth and went silently down the powder-snow slopes on nine-foot skis...Clad entirely in white, they simply vanished from sight."[27]

During the winter of 1939-40, the Finns dealt the invading Russian armies repeated defeat by attacking vital rail supply lines in the snowy mountain passes, swiftly descending like ghosts on skis bearing white death. They inflicted casualties on the enemy at a rate of 40 to 1.

Impressed by the success of these dauntless skiing freedom fighters, Charles Minot Dole --who later founded the U.S. National Ski Patrol System -- approached the U.S. Army in June, 1940, with the idea of forming a similar corps. As a result, the U.S. 87th Infantry Mtn. Regiment was activated at Fort Lewis in 1941. In the Fall of '42, Camp Hale, Colorado, became the home of the U.S. 10th Mountain Division. Their motto: "We Climb to Conquer."

In **The Military Ski Manual: A Handbook for Ski and Mountain Troops** (© 1943), Frank Harper writes:

> (Hans Schneider's Arlberg School of) deep forward knee-bend, the shift of weight to the tips of the skis, the semi-crouch as a fundamental stance in which chin, knees and toes form one line...has many notable weaknesses. One is the discarding of the telemark.

One of the single most important Allied ski missions of WWII was the daring commando raid on the Norsk Hydroelectric plant at Barren Mountain, Norway. The destruction of this facility -- whose production of heavy water was essential to Nazi experiments with nuclear fission -- helped delay Hitler's development of the atomic bomb.

The task was accomplished despite incredible odds, for the heavily fortified installation at Barren Mountain was guarded by crack S.S. troops, and protected as well by natural barriers. The complex itself lay at the bottom of a 6000-foot ravine where the sun never reached, and was surrounded by treacherous glaciers, frozen swamps and nearly impassable rivers. The unpredictable wind currents made a successful bombing raid virutally impossible.

After rigorous training in the Canadian wilderness, a specially selected team of four Norwegian saboteurs was air-dropped into position behind Barren Mountain. The Winter of '42 was the worst anyone could remember, yet the team spent five months outside, without relief, before the raid on February 23, 1943.

Joined by six British commandos on that final day, they drew up their battle orders on a wind-scoured ridge in an ice storm. Then, at midnight, the ten descended on handcrafted Canadian skis, with enough explosives and suicide pills for any eventuality. Within two hours, the installation was completely destroyed.

Although pursued by Hird storm ski-troopers, five of the Allied agents skied 350-miles to safety in Sweden. The rest continued their guerilla ski operations behind enemy lines until the end of the war.[28]

The Ski In Sport

As in ski warfare, the rivalry of competitive sport has had a profound impact on the art of skiing, and its demanding format continues to revolutionize both technology and technique for the benefit of all.

Sondre Norheim, father of the telemark turn

Although history has forgotten the names of many great competitors, Sondre Norheim is one that will be remembered forever in the annals of skiing fame. Born in 1825 at Morgedal in Telemark, Norway, Norheim is known today as the father of the telemark turn. He also designed a better binding, established incredible records for distance in jumping, and achieved a level of overall technical proficiency that made him the greatest skier of his time.

While others may have used the telemark method long before him, there is no doubt that he, more than anyone, introduced it to the world and laid the foundation for the precise system it is today.

> "This new departure (telemarking) led at once to a rapid development of the great art of jumping upon 'ski'...and there is no other branch of 'ski-lobning' which tends in the same degree to develop power of balance, control...or courage and confidence of bearing."[30]

In the dim and distant ages, Suomi might have said to Tuorda, "I think I can go faster than you." So the two would set out on a wolf hunt, each watching the pace of the other. If Suomi beat Tuorda on this particular day, Tuorda would probably try to find some way in which he could get more effort into his strides.[29]

The slalom also had its roots in Morgedal, where Norheim and companions, "made graceful turns around bushes and trees."[31] They called this *slalaam*, from *sla*: "smooth and slanting hill," and *laam*: "track."[32] In addition to jumping, "...the finished 'skilobner' must be able to do more...(including) bringing (the skis) quite round to stop short before any given obstacle...executed at full speed, that is to say, in the descent of a steep hill. In these arts the 'Telemarkingers' are complete masters..."[33]

What also made the boys from Telemark the kings-of-the-ski-hill was Norheim's invention of a superior binding to go along with his refined technique. Before 1850, the leather strap system generally used was too loose to hold the heel in place securely enough for Sondre Norheim's steered telemark.

By soaking thin birch roots in hot water to make them pliable, and then twisting them together to form a tight rope that ran from the toe-plate around the heel, he was able to achieve an unparalled degree of unity between foot and ski.[34]

In 1850, Norheim was not only able to jump sixty feet but execute the 'first' telemark turn as well, and thus "...set the style of skiing until the 1890's..."[35]

This system was made famous in 1879, when the skiers of Telemark met their rivals of Christiania (now Oslo), in a jumping competition on Husebry Hill. After the home team had shown their stuff, the visitors from Telemark took their turn...and startled the world.

> They stood erect, pliant, confident...They started with a rush, they gathered speed...and bounding out into the air, cleared 76 feet...'ere their skis touched the slippery slope below...Then they suddenly turned, stopped in a smother of snowdust, and faced the hill they had just descended. That was indeed a skiing revelation and a sight never to be forgotten...[36]

Norheim won the event, and according to one eye-witness account: "with legs drawn up he flew like a bird."[37]

To defeat their Telemark rivals, Christianians Torjus and Mikkel Hemmestveit developed their own system of skidded, wide, parallel turns known today as, 'stem-christiania' or 'christie-swing.' Likewise, Austrians -- such as Mathius Zdarsky (whose **Lilienfelder Schilauf Tecknik**, published in 1886, represents the first manual of cross-country downhill instruction ever written), and his pupil, Hans Schneider from St. Anton (whose Arlberg System of stemmed and edged turns was developed on the steep, icy slopes of the Austro-Italian frontier during WWI) -- formulated divergent techniques with great success.

Eventually, the telemark turn that had dominated the Hill in 1879 became eclipsed by a whole new way of skiing.[38] The result was a dichotomy of approach known today as alpine and nordic skiing..."a split which the revitalized telemarking style -- having come full circle -- is now resolving."[39]

From right to left: 1) Vidjetaband; 2) Elk binding; 3) Sondre Norheim's system; 4) Spanish movement binding; 5) Huitfeldts/K. *Marshall Photocopy*

TOOLS FOR THE TELEMARKER

Boots and Bindings

How to Mix, Match, Modify, Improve and Repair Them for Optimal Performance

Cross-country skiing's greatest thrills include the feeling of freedom, easy mobility and versatility its light, flexible system affords. You can go as simplified as you want, or as specialized as you need -- stripped down to body-skins for clothes, splinters for skis, tiny pieces of plastic for bindings, slippers for shoe -- and you can still telemark!

Yet, the all-around nordic skier might do well to sacrifice a certain amount of lightness in order to gain a necessary amount of control.

Telemark boots must be stiff enough to provide lateral stability at the ankle and positive pivotal torque at the ball-of-the-foot. Bindings should be relatively heavy-duty, hold the toe-area firmly in place and match boot-width to side-flange exactly (without any lateral play), to transmit turning action directly to the skis. On the other hand, the system should not be so rigid as to overly restrict forward-flexing at the ankle and ball-of-the-foot. Unless the ball-area can be pressed firmly and flatly over the ski surface, the full weight of the skier cannot be applied to the turn.

Nordic Skiing Comes To America

While the ancient cross-country approach was dying out on the alpine terrain of Europe, other intrepid descendants of the Vikings were carrying the nordic tradition to the New World. Here, both man and tool found a new nation to settle and a new home in which to grow.

Leif Erickson, the legendary Viking explorer, may actually have been the first skier in America when he landed on the shore of New England, around the year 1000 A.D.[40] Since the ski played such an important role in Norwegian life, it's likely this valuable tool was indeed carried on Erickson's voyage to the unknown; whether or not it was actually used by any members of his crew remains a mystery.

At present, credit for first ski-tracks in the United States goes instead to three of Erickson's countrymen. In 1837, Gullik Knudsen, Ole, and brother Ansten Nattestad skied across the entire breadth of Norway from their home in Numedal to set sail for the New World. According to Stein Eriksen, these immigrants "...settled in Illinois and it is known that they used skis on the Rock Prairie at Beloit near Chicago in 1841."[41]

During their ski through Norway in 1837, Knudsen and the Nattestads had shared the home of the Thorensen family in Tinn, Telemark, and upon reaching America, had written back to their former hosts with tales of adventure. The next year, the Thorensens also came to settle in the Midwest.[42] Their youngest son, John Thorensen, went on to become a skiing legend known today as 'Snowshoe' Thompson.[43]

When J. Thorensen left his new home in 1851 and headed for the California gold fields, he took with him skis like those that had crossed countless other countries and remained virtually unchanged for nearly seventy centuries.

As Bill Berry, Historian Emeritus of the U.S. Ski Association and National Ski Hall of Fame, writes:

> Skis, originally known as 'snowshoes,' became a necessity during early winters of the Gold Rush era. Introduced by Norwegians...use of the long boards spread rapidly (and) by 1860 the snowshoe was playing a leading role in the early conquest of the American West...[44]

In 1854, 'Snowshoe' Thompson struck a bargain with T.J. Matteson, of Murphey's Camp, Calavera Co., "...to continue postal service through the winter, on wages of two hundred dollars a month, no matter if the snow was twenty feet deep."[45] He was one of the first of many skiing mailmen who made it possible for communications that previously took three months (via clippership from the East Coast around South America), to instead reach San Francisco over the mountains in only twelve days.

Carrying a fifty-pound pack of mail on 25 lb. skis of oak he made himself,[46] 'Snowshoe' Thompson crossed the Sierras between Placerville, California and Carson Valley, Nevada in

the dead of winter -- alone -- for twenty years.[47]

According to a report in "Hutching's California Magazine's" February, 1857 issue, the technique of these mailmen was similar to that depicted in 5000-year old stone etchings:

> Upon descending surfaces they run with great ease and rapidity, and when the declivity is very great, (it is) necessary to check the motion by throwing the weight of the (skier) upon a double-handed staff, six feet in length, forced into the snow upon one side.[48]

Even today, with equipment and technique far more refined, 'Snowshoe' Thompson's record would be difficult to match. Yet, his incredible success over decades of constant peril proves that courage, stamina, confidence and experience are the most important qualities a backcountry skier can possess. His spirit -- like his example -- still survives. Buried in Genoa, Nevada, 'Snowshoe Thompson' is commemorated by a gravestone bearing crossed skis and the epitaph: "Gone but not forgotten."[49]

Nor are others of Thompson's time forgotten, contemporaries who 'toured' the mountains of the American West during the Gold Rush era. The Reverand John L. Dyer, an itinerant Methodist preacher (born March 15, 1812), carried the mail between camps in Colorado via the 13,000-foot Buckskin Joe-California Gulch trail.

He is credited with saving several skiless miners trapped in the deep powder of the high country, as well as faithfully carrying both news from home and the word of God to the isolated souls who worked the wilderness.[50] In **Snowshoe Itinerant**, his own account, Dyer writes: "My snowshoes were of Norwegian style, from nine to eleven-feet in length...I carried a pole."[51]

During this period, cross-country downhill competition became an American sport. As early as 1854, Porter's Woodturning Shop in California was producing skis. That same year, racers competed in the Lost Sierra/Lake Tahoe Miner's Downhill -- a contest with no turns.

The original Winter Sports Association, called the "Alturas Snowshoe Club," was formed in LaPorte, California in 1867.[52] In 1874, Tommy Todd is said to have won the LaPorte Race over an 1,804-foot downhill course with a time of 14 seconds. If true, Todd would thus have averaged a speed of 88 miles per hour![53]

Perhaps the greatest downhiller of the times in the Rocky Mountain region was Al Johnson, whose story is best told by Western State College Professor and Colorado Historian, Dr. Duane Vandenbusche:

The Great Snowshoer Of the Gunnison Country

He was a legend in the 1880's and 1890's in the Gunnison country and he has stayed a legend. Today, he is enshrined in the Colorado Ski Hall of Fame at Vail, one of the ten charter members of that illustrious club. His name was Al Johnson. He and his brother Fred were from eastern Canada, where they learned to ski as young boys. As early as the 1870's both had become superb skiers and had competed in ski races in the St. Laurentian Mountains near Quebec.

The lure of gold and silver led the Johnson brothers to the Gunnison country from Canada in 1880. Making their way across the continent by rail into Denver, the brothers rode mules into Crested Butte, the "Gateway to the Elk Mountains," in early 1880.

From Crested Butte, Al Johnson and his brother trekked north along the East River, over Schofield Pass and finally to the banks of the Crystal River fifteen miles away, where a booming silver camp called Crystal had been laid out. It was a route that Al Johnson would get to know well and make famous.

Beginning in early November of 1880, Johnson was hired to carry the mail between Crested Butte and Crystal, summer and winter. During the winter months, the trip was frightfully hazardous. From Crystal, Johnson had to make his way through Crystal Canyon and past the famed "Devil's Punchbowls" -- which struck fear into the heart of any sane man. The canyon's steep and glassy walls regularly vomitted avalanches into the sheer ravine below, making winter travel almost impossible.

Johnson knew that many a miner had been killed by rock and snowslides in the narrow chasm. The steep vertical sides of Crystal Canyon were notorious for unleashing tremendous avalanches into the Crystal River below. But the mail had to go through!

Sucking in his breath, while he said a silent prayer that he would not fall, Johnson pushed himself forward into the Crystal Canyon and, "turned them loose." He could not falter.

Crouching low with guide pole in hand, the Canadian snowshoer picked up tremendous speed in the tracks he had made the previous day. A ski race was one thing, but Al Johnson literally was skiing for his life -- he had to stand. Only his early training in Canada, and his nerves of steel, enabled him to stay alive and get the mail through.

The Nansen Ski Club of Berlin, New Hampshire (named for the great explorer, Fridtjof Nansen), was founded in 1883,[54] but unlike the professionalism of the West, "skiing in the East (was) a sport for the amateur, as it was for the most part under the domination of colleges and universities."[55]

For example, Fred H. Harris, "who learned to ski as a sophomore in high school with nine-foot skis, matriculated at Dartmouth College in the class of 1911. After he became oriented to his surroundings, he produced a pair of ski and made mysterious tracks in hills and vales around the village of Hanover, New Hampshire."[56] He also founded the famous Dartmouth College Outing Club in 1910. Their annual Winter Carnival, which featured relay races, jumping and uphill-downhill competitions, led to the first intercollegiate ski meet in 1914.[57]

That year, according to one account:

> A great crowd assembled at the Vale of Tempe, where the ski-jumping contest was held...Starting far above, at a given signal, the jumper speeds with ever-increasing velocity toward the take-off. A scant few yards away, he crouches, and as the brink is reached, hurls himself out erect and well-balanced, into the space beyond. Then follows the hiss of the jumper's body as it passes through the air, shooting out and down, landing lightly on the slope below, then rushing out on the level plain beneath, to swerve suddenly, send up a cloud of snow, and end abruptly in a beautifully executed telemark swing.[58]

Today, Crested Butte, Colorado -- a National Historic District surrounded by 14,000-foot peaks in the Southcentral portion of the state -- is considered the capitol of telemark turning. It was here, on the same slopes Al Johnson traversed one-hundred years before, that Doug Buzzell, Craig Hall, Greg Dalbey, Jack Marcial, Rick Borkovec and other outstanding local skiers went about rediscovering the almost forgotten turn in the early 1970's.

Borkovec, who is currently director of the

The Paradise Divide of Crested Butte, Co./*Patrick Hickey Photo*

Nordic Adventure Ski School at Crested Butte Mountain Resort, describes his initial experiments with CBMR Pro Patrolmen Rob Hunker and Steve Allen:

> Standing on the groomed slopes of the area, looking out at the backcountry, we longed to ski those untouched runs far from the crowded lifts. I felt this desire could be fulfilled through cross-country skiing, and in 1971 I began to seriously explore the backcountry potential of nordic equipment.
> We soon found that conventional downhill techniques were generally unsuited to the racing skis we first used, or the conditions we encountered. The snowplow didn't work very well for us in deep powder, and the parallel turn seemed too unstable on free-heeled binding and flexible boots.
> We eventually worked out the basics of the telemark, guided by an old picture I had seen of Stein Eriksen's father demonstrating the turn, and went from there on our own.
> The rest, as they say, is history.

This group of Crested Butte three-pinners, led by Jack Marcial, also formed the original Ski to Die Club, and their combined expertise and daring, innovative approach pushed the very limits of nordic capability in progressively more radical terrains. Of course, when "extreme skiing" is defined as, "If you fall, you die" (Chris Landry), neither the telemark technique nor cross-country equipment will probably ever provide the level of control offered by alpine gear.

Yet, the telemark descents these and other skiers are accomplishing have earned them the respect of their alpine peers, and converted many a skeptic along the way. Their spirit has spread the sport once again to all corners of the globe, and telemarking's current popularity is probably greater than at any other time in history.

> Little did this group...realize that their counter-culture skiing technique...would lead to a...telemark renaissance...Its growing popularity marks the end of an era of overspecialization, and for many telemarking is ultimately the most versatile and useful form of skiing around.[59]

Marius Eriksen/
*Reprinted from
Stein Eriksen's*
Come Ski with Me

Brad Makoff taking off on a 175-foot leap/*Photo by Gus Mora, killed by an avalanche in Todd's Bowl, Park City West, March, 1982.*

III TELEMARK TURNING TODAY THE FUN- DAMENTALS

You cannot learn to fly by flying.
First you must learn to walk,
And to run, and to climb,
And to dance.

Nietzsche

After soaring for hundreds of meters in distance, high above the ground, nordic jumpers land their long skis with amazing precision and grace. To absorb the shock of their downward momentum and maintain balance, they often assume a straight-running telemark stance. Initiated gradually just prior to touchdown and emphatically completed at the instant of impact, this movement acts to dissipate the force of compression, and allows the flier to land in total control.

Whether you're dropping out of the sky after a thirty-second hang-time, plowing through changing conditions on the flat, negotiating a sharp dip or abrupt rise in varying terrain, you too can use this same technique to make difficult transitions smoothly on skinny skis and free-heeled bindings.

Beyond its advantage of supple stability, the telemark stance is also a stepping-stone to the more complex telemark turn. By mastering this fundamental straight-running position from the very beginning, you'll progress rapidly and correctly to advanced skills. Likewise, when you think you've learned it all, you've ceased to learn, while further refinement of the rudiments can add a whole new level of expertise to your wildest free-skiing abilities.

As Amund Ekroll, head coach of the Professional Ski Instructors' International Nordic Demonstration Team, advises: "Until you can do the simplest technique one-thousand times without mistake -- indeed, unless you never make a mistake -- you haven't really learned the technique." In this way, fundamentals become both the beginning and the end, the very essence of, 'total telemarking.'

So, instead of jumping off a 90-meter cliff to learn the telemark turn, let's start with the basics.

General Principles of Dynamic Action

Telemark skiing is incredibly dynamic, combining form and fluidity, speed and timing, rhythm and control, power and grace to link movements over uneven, frozen terrain. The object, of course, is to stay standing, never as easy as it sounds on skinny skis.

Balance, Form and Centeredness

The often complex sequence of actions involved in skiing must be executed on several different planes at the same time.[1] Thus, balance depends to a great degree on a powerful and flexible form.

Your lower body is constantly driving forward, compressing and extending beneath you while supporting your overall weight in the radically lowered position of the telemark.

Your legs must therefore be strong enough to hold a stable stance, yet elastic enough to shift quickly in accordance with the ever-changing conditions of slope and snow.

While your legs do most of the work in telemark skiing, your upper body should also be strong and supple. Your head, shoulders, and chest must sit firmly over your base area to positively weight your skis, and yet staying within the parameters which define overall balance requires flexibility.

Your arms and poles also provide forceful leverage and added stability when trekking or turning, yet, like the torso, should remain as relaxed and motionless as possible.

Your midsection, or abdominal region, links upper and lower body sections together, transmitting energy from one to the other through the bone and musculature of the hips. Because of their mass and might, the hips generate a tremendous amount of power when applied to any action.

Just as the driveshaft of a wheel creates a greater and faster movement on the outer circle than at the center, a given amount of rotation by the hips produces a greater amount of motion at the body's extremities.[2]

The midsection also contains your *center of gravity*, the inner balance point of your overall mass. This area, located within the sphere of the abdomen (about 1½-inches below and behind the navel), is also the focal point for all external forces acting upon the skier's body.

Thus, the *position of the midsection* plays a critical role in the stability of your form. The lower your center of gravity and the wider your base, the more solid your stance. In order to **move quickly in any direction, though, you** need a slightly narrower stance and higher center. Likewise, if your midsection strays too far outside the area of your base, you'll fall.

On the other hand, every *movement of the body* alters the point of balance, requiring another movement to regain a position of centeredness. To achieve the degree of coordination necessary in dynamic skiing, Denis Hall advises: "Instead of attempting to *hold* your center in any one place, it is more useful to know where your center *is* at all times."

By subtly adjusting the various parts of the body around the pivotal of your constantly shifting midpoint, your form harmonizes with -- rather than reacts to -- the forces of nature, allowing you to flow smoothly down the fall line.

To many cultures, the midsection is considered the *center of spirit*, as well as the center of mass. Here is thought to reside another source of power, an inner strength known as prana (Hindu), chi (Chinese), or ki (Japanese), which is said to be an embodiment of the universal life-force. Although difficult to describe, ki manifests itself when the power of the will works in complete cooperation with the strength of the body, so that the total energy of one's being is focused on a single goal.

Ki is often employed unconsciously by people in times of extreme emergency, when the instinct for survival automatically overcomes the accepted limitations of body and mind. There are many recorded instances which clearly illustrate this phenomenon, such as the case of the mother who manages to lift the front-end of a truck to free her child trapped beneath. Through practice and proper attitude, everyone is capable of tapping the power of this force.

I first became acquainted with the concept of ki in 1971, when I began the study of Shodokan Karate under Master Kazumi Tabata. The awesome power of this Oriental is belied by his 5'7" frame, but is quite obvious in his every action. When standing stationary, he seems to be as rooted to the earth as the trunk of a tree, yet when he moves he seems to flow like water, as if his form is being pulled across the floor by an invisible string attached to his midsection.

In my subsequent years of training in the martial arts, I have come to understand that these qualities are a direct result of the application of ki, and I have found strikingly similar examples of its use by expert athletes in other disciplines. At the very least, the total telemarker should be aware that ki exists as a power source of immense potential.

Speed and timing are also important aspects of dynamic form. Strength is only effective if used correctly, and must be applied quickly and at just the right moment in order to focus maximum force with minimum effort. Sensei Tabata defines "power" as the combination of speed, form and focus (mental, physical and spiritual concentration).

> There is timing in everything...without it there is neither harmony nor rhythm. Timing is the essence of all skills and abilities...
> You must be able to discern and utilize the patterns of timing...You must integrate your position within the overall pattern of changes, otherwise your strategy will become uncertain...
>
> *Musashi, "Ring of Earth"*

Likewise, proper breathing is necessary for the stamina required in extended situations, as well as the effortless fluidity which marks the really good skiers on any slope. The average person uses only a portion of the lungs' capacity, filling the top-halves but not the bottoms during inhalation, and never quite emptying all the stale air when exhaling. During sleep, however, we naturally use our entire volume of intake.

This same ability can be developed by practicing controlled-breathing exercises. Concentrate on visualizing the stream of oxygen as imaginary smoke circulating through your system. Breathe it in steadily through both nose and partially-opened mouth. Then close your windpipe, and force the trapped air deep into your lungs by constricting your abdominal muscles slightly while pressing down with your diaphram.

Hold in the breathe momentarily, imagining the smoke swirling around at the bottom of your lungs. You can actually feel when you have filled them completely. Then exhale, visualizing the smoke trailing smoothly out from your nose and mouth. Just when you think you've emptied your lungs completely, press down with your diaphram again to squeeze out the last measure of dead air. Pause, then inhale and repeat the procedure.

Try to establish a controlled, yet natural tempo. At first, you'll probably gulp and pant, but with time you'll learn to relax and become completely comfortable with this new and better method of respiration.

Once you've mastered it in a resting situation, you can apply it to dynamic skiing. Generally, you should exhale during the active phase -- when you initiate a movement -- and inhale during the passive phase of the biomechanic sequence.

Just as tennis champion, Jimmy Connors, exhales with an audible grunt each instant that his racquet makes contact with the ball, so the nordic skier will breathe out emphatically with each stride or turn.

When ski-climbing in high-altitude conditions or on steep terrain, proper breathing will not only establish rhythm and pace (so important to a 'mountaineers' stride'), but help conserve energy as well.

Getting Strong and Staying Loose

Before starting any activity, I recommend you spend at least ten minutes warming up your muscles by stretching from head to foot. Static exercises are best, and bouncing movements should be avoided, since they tend to strain non-elastic tendons and ligaments, as well as cause some muscles to contract instead of relax. "Not only does a static stretch workout warm you up and improve your efficient strength, it also has a powerful relaxation effect, and that relaxation is essential in helping you concentrate."[3]

Bob Anderson's, **Stretching**, is the classic reference on the subject; this book and others will tell you all you need to know about proper stretching.

While stretching can strengthen and coordinate your overall body, it doesn't hurt to throw in a few power exercises to develop specific telemark muscles. After you've loosened up, for example, try doorway squats, toe

The author demonstrating an exaggerated diagonal stride/ Nathan Bilow Photo

raises, and bunny hops.

If you really want to keep your legs in tip-top telemark trim, try:

backcountry bicycling, or

summer climbing and downhill running with poles.

Cross-country ski running is another excellent way to develop supple limbs, strong muscles and long wind. If there's one thing instructors of nordic technique seem to agree on, it is: the telemark turn is an extension of the nordic stride, which is an extension of running, which is an extension of walking. By sharpening rhythm and fluidity as well, ski touring is a perfect way to compliment and improve your telemark skills.

Nordic Diagonal Stride

Stride down the level track by bounding off one ski while driving the other ahead. Rather than kicking down and back, think of this action as a forward explosion: an emphatic thrust of body-mass completely to the front leg. The rear leg is extended naturally behind, with the ski-tail lifted partially off the snow to accentuate total forward weight-shift.

At the same time, working in harmony with the rhythm of the legs, your arms drive in the opposite manner: as your right ski moves ahead, your left (or diagonally-opposed), hand reaches forward -- just as if you were running. The right arm extends naturally to the rear, crossing (or 'breaking'), the vertical plane of the body. The difference between this action and running is that the skier glides between each stride in a resting phase, and gains additional momentum from the leverage of the poling action in the driving phase.

The Dynamic Telemark Stance

After loosening up, assume a *straight-running telemark position* and hold it. Start by taking a *natural stance*: spread your feet (with or without skis), to the sides, shoulder-width apart, and bend your knees slightly.

Your entire posture should be upright and centered: back straight, head up and eyes looking forward, shoulders square and level, weight evenly distributed over both feet. Hold your arms relaxed and naturally out from your sides, with hands held about hip-level and slightly forward. Focus your inner attention on your body position, and your outward attention -- not at your feet -- but several yards ahead. In other words, *look where you're going and feel where you're at.*

Now, take about a 24-inch step ahead with one foot, leaving the other in place, and drop into a low telemark: drive your knees forward, flex your ankles and sink straight down with your hips. (Modern American telemark technique has shortened the distance between the two skis fore-and-aft, but 24-inches is a good average).

In the telemark position, the forward leg is bent at a 45-degree angle, with the knee held directly over a flat and evenly-weighted front foot. The rear leg is also bent at a 45-degree angle, but your heel is raised and weight rests solely on the ball of the back foot.

Bounce up and down lightly with your hips, and rock back and forth with your ankles and knees until you find a position of centeredness and your weight is distributed evenly between both feet. Relax your toes, and feel your feet inside your boots. Concentrate on pressing your weight firmly and flatly across the entire bearing surface of each.

The telemark stance; front view/Brad English illustration

As Jim Thomas, member of the Crested Butte Ski to Die Club, recommends: "Ski as if you were bare-footed." Working in conjunction with the eyes (your center of visual reference), and the ears (which help determine your rate of speed by the sound of air passing their outer lobes, and whose inner semi-circular canals act as a gauge of levelness), the sole of the feet serve as centers of balance. They sense subtle variations in speed, snow or terrain, and transmit appropriate movements to the skis.

This is what Jean-Claude Killy calls, "the intelligence of the feet,"[5] and is one of the keys to skiing finesse. The greater sensitivity of cross-country boots will help develop this awareness, and also devout alpine skiers can improve their balance and edge control by practicing on nordic gear.

Even with the lightest of boots, though, distributing 50 percent of your weight over the ball of your rear foot in the telemark position isn't as easy as it sounds, but at times is absolutely essential. Here is a learning-aid, developed by RMSIA Nordic certification examiner, Rick Borkovec, that may help:

At home, assume a telemark position in your ski boots, with a bathroom scale placed beneath your rear foot. Adjust your stance forward and backward until half your total body weight is registered on the scale. You'll probably be surprised to discover how much pressure is actually needed on the rear foot to achieve equal weight distribution. Concentrate on remembering what it feels like when you are in this position of centeredness, then switch feet and without looking at the scale try to duplicate the proper stance.

Once you are accustomed to driving into a

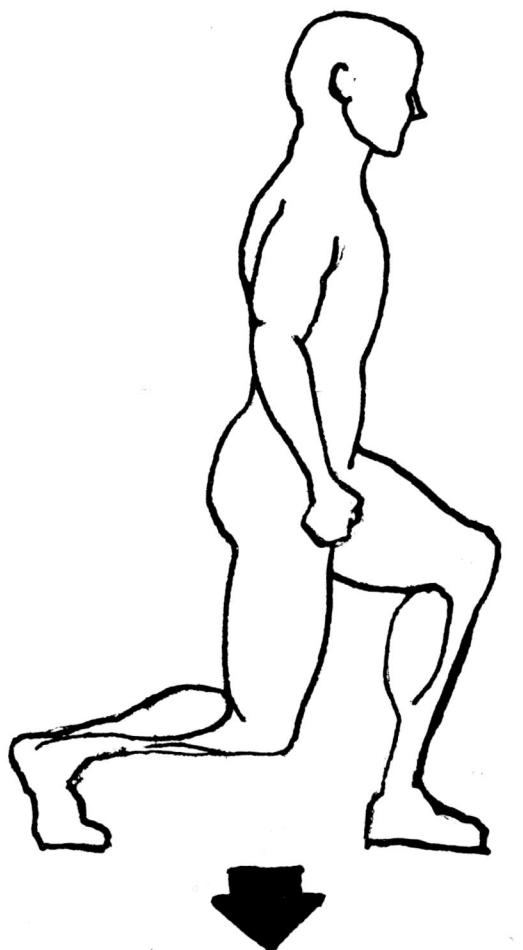

The telemark stance; side/B. English illustration

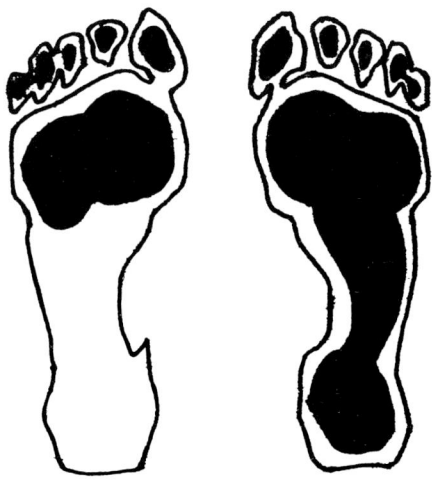

Distribution of weight in telemark stance

solid and centered telemark position, practice moving from one telemark right into another. Start on flat ground, first without, and then with skis. In many conditions, I like to keep my midsection traveling along as even a plane as possible, without excessive 'bobbing,' or up-down motion as I change the position of my feet and skis.

Rather than thrusting up and out of a low telemark into another, try shifting your weight forward by driving your knees and drawing your hips ahead. Roll naturally at your ankles -- as if rocking from the back foot to the front without lifting either off the ground.

At the same time, slide your rear ski forward, keeping enough weight on it so it stays in contact with the snow. As it passes beneath your midsection, and moves ahead of the body's vertical axis, begin to weight both skis evenly again.

Next, try straight-running downhill in the telemark position, without any turns or lead changes from top to bottom. Find a short hill with a long, flat run-out: one that's steep enough so you don't have to pole, yet gentle enough to keep your speed manageable. Pick a clear area, away from rocks and trees, where the snow is neither deep nor crusty. Stand at the top and face right down the fall line in a natural stance, not a telemark stance, with skis parallel and shoulder-width apart. Push off and pick up a little speed in this position. The object is to get used to driving emphatically into a telemark instead of starting from a tentative stance and inching stiffly forward. Once you've gained some momentum, stride and sink: slide one ski straight ahead just as you did on the flat, drop your hips and bend your knees. Press hard on both feet, stay relaxed and hold your balance to the bottom. Don't even think about falling; just concentrate on shifting your weight and staying on your feet as the slope demands.

Herringbone or side-step back up the slope and try it again. When you can stride into, and hold, a straight-running telemark position with control from top to bottom, go ahead and put several telemark transitions together. See how many times you can move smoothly from one

TOOLS FOR THE TELEMARKER

Protective Kneepads

In contrast to alpine skiing, nordic-related injuries are rare -- partly because of the equipment, and partly because of the terrain involved in its basic approach. Telemark skiing is also relatively safe, but is not without hazards.

As cross-country downhill boots become more rigid in design, and skiers continue to tackle more radical situations, such injuries as boot-top (ankle) fractures, upper leg breaks, shoulder separations, spinal compressions (head-plant-type falls), and knee damage are becoming more common.

Because the telemark stance places the knees in a vulnerable low and critically angled position in relation to the ground, 'knee-bashing' is another potential problem. While little can be done to prevent torn ligaments other than cautious skiing, kneepads can help reduce fractures of the patela or other impact-related traumas to the knee area.

Early and late season telemark skiing is especially hazardous, since the thin snowpack increases the chance of your crashing into boulders or stumps lurking just beneath the surface. Keeping your knees directly over your skis at all times, as Bob (B.C.) Vandervoort recommends, is one way to avoid these threats, but there's still the problem of the rear knee smashing down onto the binding or ski itself -- particularly if you're telemarking through difficult conditions or mogul-filled slopes.

While they may seem like elitist paraphenalia, kneepads are essential items for telemark skiing, and I highly recommend both beginners and experts wear them at all times. You never know when you'll wind up doing a few turns, but if you hit something without kneepads, you'll probably wind up in the hospital.

A wrestling-style variety works well and is available in most sporting-goods stores for under $10.00.

Stride, freeze and sink/*Paul Gallaher Photos*

position to the other.

Of course, different conditions require different techniques, and there are times when you should make your transition from one telemark stance to the other very emphatically. An exercise taught by professional instructor and helicopter ski guide, Eric Sanford, at his outstanding Telemark Camp in Mazama, Washington, will help you develop this skill.

Start without poles on flat, packed snow, and take three diagonal strides forward. Concentrate on shifting all your weight to your front ski in one explosive motion, swinging your opposite hand forward at the same time. Pause between each stride and let your skis glide for awhile. Make each motion smoothly; don't rush!

On the third stride, hold your position in mid-glide and then drop into a straight-running telemark crouch. This sequence follows a definite cadence that can be recited to yourself: *"Diagonal stride...stride...stride... Freeze! and sink."* On the word *"Freeze!,"* your arms and legs stop their pendulum-swing and your hands stay right where they are. On *"sink,"* straighten up your forward-leaning torso and just drop your hips.

Repeat the sequence for three more beats, driving up-and-out of your lowered stance into a diagonal stride: stride, pause, stride, pause, stride and sink. Now you'll end up with your other ski in the lead, and opposite hand forward.

Once you've established a comfortable rhythm, practice moving from one telemark stance right into another: *"Stride...freeze and telemark; stride...freeze and telemark..."*

Now, try this with poles, but don't get confused! At first, don't even plant them. Keep your hand-grips pointed ahead with your

baskets to the rear, poles swinging freely off the snow. Don't wave them out to the sides; instead, keep them brushing against your hips and following the same line of travel as your skis: straight ahead.

When you **do** use your poles, the forward one is planted after the pause between strides, when your gliding momentum ends and your driving thrust is begun. Maintain the pole's backward angle, plant, and push back as you explode forward. Your hand should follow through to the rear so that your poling arm passes beyond the line of your body. Think of yourself as reaching back with one arm and leg as well as reaching ahead with the others. Try not to let your poling action interrupt the natural rhythm of your stride.

A common tendency is to concentrate too much on the poling action until you find your arms and legs out of syncopation. Watch out for pass-ganging (parallel-poling), or the mistake of having both right hand and right ski forward at the same time.

If you find yourself tipping from side to side, widen your stance from side-to-side instead of jabbing with your poles.

Like the rhythm of diagonal striding, the telemark turn emphasizes an alternate arm-swing and leg-drive motion. The only difference is that during the turn your forward ski is directed at an angle to your rear ski, both are edged, and your weight is low and equal over both feet. By following the curve of a circle with your front foot while practicing the diagonal stride on the flat, you will naturally initiate a turn. In his innovative book, **Cross-Country Downhill and Other Nordic Mountain Skiing Techniques**, published in 1978 by Pacific Search Press, Steve Barnett describes this exercise as "the crooked stride."

Diagonal stride into telemark/ B. English

From here, striding into a telemark turn on the slope is just like dancing down stairs. Start on a gentle hill. Take a gradual traverse instead of aiming straight down, and turn up into the hill rather than around the fall line.

Simply diagonal stride for a few beats to establish a smooth tempo and generate momentum, drop over the knoll of the hill, stride your downhill ski forward at an angle to your rear ski, sink and hold your telemark to a stop. In otherwords, from a gradual downhill traverse: *Diagonal stride...Stride...Crooked stride...Freeze and sink.*

Turning Dynamics: Body and Ski

Like all ski techniques, the mechanics of the telemark involve the dynamic and passive turning forces of body and ski: a carving action of the tools initiated by the will and power of the skier. Its fundamental aspects combine:
- The body's movements to pivot the skis in the new direction;
- The skis' inherent tendency to arc once correctly directed;
- Muscular control of the forces in motion by the driving of the lower body and the overall distribution of pressure on the skis throughout the turning phases.

Phase I: Initiation

A. The pivoting action is only possible with an unweighted ski; thus, the skier must begin a turn by an emphatic shift of the center of mass (CM) over the skis.
  1. This unweighting process can be achieved by:
    a. Up-unweighting
    b. Down-unweighting
    c. Edge-set/rebound
    d. Pole-planting
    e. etc.
B. Once unweighted, the skis are twisted into the turn primarily by the power of the muscles of the lower body:
  1.a. The feet change leads
    b. The feet steer
    c. The hips rotate
    d. The knees drive
  2. The knees, as Denis Hall advises, "can

be envisioned as organic gyroscopes: you point them where you want to go, then follow them." Unless they are properly aligned, however, their guiding power will not be effectively transmitted to the skis. Think of your lower leg as a single leverage unit: the vertical plane of the foot, ankle and knee unbroken. In other words, don't let your knees 'flop' to the inside or outside.

    a. Apply this force to your turning ski by pointing your knee slightly inward, pressing along the inside edge of your downhill boot with your big toe, and pressing outward (counter), with your heel.

    b. The rear leg and foot also steer in the same direction, but less emphatically.

Phase II· Control

A. Once initiated, the turning action can be controlled by the continued steering of the feet and driving of the knees, combined with adjustment of the **CM** over the activated skis

B. The degree of forward/backward weight distribution, and lateral lean of the upper body depend on the nature of the conditions at hand and the type of turn desired;

C. Generally, the **CM** is shifted primarily to the newly-leading (outside), ski during the initiation phase; secondly, more equally over both during the control phase; and finally, most positively to the rear ski during the completion of the turn;

D. The important thing to remember is that the turning forces of the legs and skis are more effective than that of the upper body, resulting in quicker, more concise and less tiring technique.

Phase III: Finish

A. Once the skis have passed the fall line, the turn is completed by one, or a combination of actions:
    1. Emphatic heel check, or tail-thrust;
    2. Reduced steering;
    3. Reduced edging.

Turning Dynamics
Poling Action

A. The abrupt leverage of a planted pole adds another turning force to the pivoting action, while the static position of the hands helps control direction and radius of the turn.

B. "If the upper body is blocked with a solid pole plant, all of the turning power is transferred to the legs."[6]

C. The pole plant provides a positive impulse for unweighting, and the hands act as pointers steering a constant path for the upper body down the fall line.

Anticipation

Since your skis tend to follow the direction of your upper body, avoid swinging your arms too far across the slope (perpendicular to fall line), or your skis will probably over-turn. Both ski-tails will drop downhill, or 'wash-out' behind you, leaving you facing uphill and in no position to start a new turn.

Instead, use the fall line as a reference in your descent, and then direct yourself ahead

Left: Anticipation of the upper body/B. English

Right: The coiled-spring effect of anticipation/ B. English

by keeping your upper body facing down your chosen path at all times. By anticipating -- this *facing down the path with your mind and center* -- you are looking, thinking and preparing for the next pitch or turn. You are in a position of readiness, able to respond quickly without unecessary motion which might upset balance and timing.

As Georges Joubert, author of **How to Ski the French Way**, and, **Teach Yourself to Ski**, defines it:

> Anticipation is either a pivoted position of the upper body in the direction of the upcoming turn before its initiation, or it is a pivoting movement which results in this position.

Anticipation also creates a 'coiled-spring effect.' By rotating your torso counter to your skis, tension is built up through the framework of your midsection to your feet in the form of potential energy. When you unweight your skis, and release this stored tension, your legs will naturally uncoil in the direction of the new turn: the direction your upper body is facing.

"Anticipation is a turning of the hips combined with a forward bending of the torso in the direction of the oncoming turn before its initiation to create muscle tension."

"Another strong point...is that it allows the skier (especially during shorter, linked turns) to remain facing in the general direction of travel and not upset the quiet movements of torso and center of gravity." (Horst Abrams, "Terminology," **Journal of Pro Ski Instruction**, Vol. 3, p. 32 (Boulder: © 1980, PSIA)).

PSIA examiner, Rick Borkovec, has developed a simple and effective way to learn anticipation with a partner.

Counting Fingers Throughout a Turn

One person (whom we'll call teacher), stands part-way down the practice hill, while the other person begins to link turns from above, aimed in the general direction of the teacher. Teacher holds up his hand and raises any number of fingers. The student must watch the hand closely while turning, and call out the correct number of fingers displayed. Teacher continues to change the number of fingers, and student must keep his head and eyes focused down the fall line in an anticipating position in order to 'pass the test.'

Angulation

When traversing or turning on steep or icy pitches, I sometimes find myself leaning awkwardly into the slope, using my uphill pole as a crutch planted in the snow to keep me from falling.

Even though this 'pole-stabbing' may work as an emergency survival technique, it indicates that my weight is not centered over my edges. I may remain standing, but my turns will be sloppy and ineffective.

To avoid this problem yourself, try angulating for better balance on steep slopes and sharper, carved turns in any condition.

As your feet, ankles and knees drive into the slope to set your edges, tuck in with your hips and tilt out and down the fall line with your upper body, instead of leaning into the hill.

This will keep your head and shoulders plumb over your feet, enabling direct transfer of weight through your hips to the inside edge of your downhill ski for increased holding power throughout the turning action.

Practice by standing on flat ground and inclining your legs and knees to one side, as if edging. Notice how your torso naturally tips the other way, to bring your head in line with your feet and maintain balance.

Similarly, when you lose your footing while walking on slick ice, you will automatically angulate in an attempt to recover balance: you'll 'jack-knife' emphatically at your waist to bring your head back over your feet.

Angulation of the feet, ankles and knees, either separately or as a unit, creates an edging effect on your skis. Angulation is also a method of shifting your torso to a more centered position, improving balance as well as edging power. The hips twist (rotate), toward the inside of the turn, while tipping (bending), out and down the fall line.

The angulation of Clifton Garland/Jim Kahnweiler Photo

Tom Carr on the steep and icy slopes of Pico de Orizaba, Mexico's 18,700-foot volcano, during the first nordic descent of the third highest peak in North America; Thanksgiving, 1981/*Mike Carr Photo*

IV SPECIAL CONDITIONS/ ADVANCED TECHNIQUE

"Nordic 'Pre-Turn Ideas,'" By Paul Parker, PSIA Nordic Examiner and member of the U.S. Nordic Demo Team.

An idea useful in nordic skiing is that of the "pre-turn," a direct carry over from alpine technique. In simple terms, this means setting an edge to create a platform from which to initiate your next turn. This can be done in several positions.

Most common is a telemark position edge-set, followed by a hard switch into the next turn. I've found, however, that on steep terrain, and when carrying a pack, the alpine-style, parallel pre-turn is preferable.

As I finish one turn I bring the skis together, parallel technique, then edge-set and step into the telemark lead for the next turn.

This helps to eliminate that feeling of terminal velocity in a long radius turn that doesn't want to end --when you are, in fact, quite anxious to get going in another direction.[1]

Arctic sastrugie encountered during the first descent of Labrador's 4,550 foot Mt. Grange/ *Peter Dea Photo*

A radical step-telemark by Don Cook in crud/ *Doug Pierson Photos*

Step Telemark

The key to handling difficult conditions, as Parker suggests, is a matter of getting the skis around the turn as quickly as possible. Here's another technique -- first described by Steve Barnett -- which was developed by Crested Butte, Colorado skiers on hard-packed mogul fields, yet works well in many other situations.

From a compressed stance, with edge-set, stride vigorously into a right-hand turn by *stepping across the fall line* with your left ski. Simply walk over your downhill ski and shift weight completely to your left foot -- which is angled in the direction of the new turn. Then step the right ski around and slap it down in line with the now-leading left ski. Weight both skis again in a low telemark, and complete the turn. Thinking about *stepping the rear ski back,* as well as into, the telemark position will help you regain a secure stance.

Stem Telemark

In some conditions you'll want to move emphatically to the front ski, and in others -- like variably breakable crust -- you'll want to change leads as gently as possible. That's when a sliding stem turn often works best. This technique, taught by Don Portman at the Trak Telemark Camp in Mazama, Washington, gets you quickly yet smoothly around the fall line and enables slow, controlled skiing in many tricky situations.

To turn left, ease the right, uphill ski out over the snow into a telemark wedge, with the lead tip pointed in the direction of the turn. Shift all your weight onto this ski, which, in crust, means breaking through completely. Next, lift the tail of the rear ski out of the snow and step it around the fall line along side the downhill ski. Then drop your hips to the telemark position, and weight that back ski. Come to a complete stop. Pause and repeat the sequence.

Lateral Projection

For quicker, shorter turns than are possible using a diagonal stride telemark in steep terrain, resort to the telemark step turn utilizing lateral projection...

Skiing across the fall line of the hill with ski weighted equally, plant your downhill pole;

1. Step off your downhill ski, projecting your weight onto the inside edge of your uphill ski...

2. Continue to edge your uphill ski, carving the turn into the fall line, all the while bringing your downhill ski in line in preparation for the telemark...

3. When the uphill ski is positioned, distribute your weight equally over both skis and drive the ski through the turn with your knee and foot. Wayne Hanson, *Cross-Country Downhill,* **Cross-Country Skier Magazine,** November 1981, p. 34

Two-Step Telemark

Here's an even faster way to initiate turns on the super steep: From a traverse, to the left, first step the downhill ski directly into the fall line. Pause. Next, step across (in front of), this one with the other. Shift weight completely onto the now-leading left ski. Then, bring the rear ski around, sink down over both and steer. This initial scissoring action puts you momentarily in the fall line, but don't panic. Instead, retain your composure and make each step precisely before going on to the next. Concentrate on vigorous up-unweighting with positive forward striding, and follow through with a definite down-weighting action.

Two-step telemark/*Paul Gallaher Photos*

Open turn/
Eric Burr
Illustration

Open Turns and Telemarking
by Eric Burr

The stemmed telemark turn pushes legs, skis, and body together into a secure position allowing an extremely low center of gravity. As currently taught in American ski schools, the feet are only about one-quarter ski-length apart, as opposed to the old half ski length or full telemark. This enables faster recoveries: the rear ski actually slides down the side of a furrow created by the first ski at either full or half telemark. This adds another turning force to the telemark beyond what any other turn can offer. As snow squeezes skis, legs, and body together, it also rotates the skier with a center of gravity in-between the bindings. The only *openess* required is that of extending the upper arm forward and the lower arm back, to better balance over the skis and honestly face the drop ahead.

The most efficient way to turn nordic skis downhill is usually not the stemmed telemark. Secure maybe, but efficient, no. The carved parallel in a telemark position gets that honor, leaving behind it the narrowest tracks in skiing. Any angling of moving skis in relation to each other produces drag. The telemark is just one way to convert this drag into rotary movement.

The other way is with *scissored, or open turns*. Scissored skis still drag, but they drag outside edges as opposed to the stem's inside edges. Counteracting this drag requires that legs be pulled together, resisting the snow's tendency to pull them apart.

The most successful teaching sequence I've discovered is to start students out in gentle traverses on smooth, well-groomed slopes, first lifting then pushing ahead with the uphill ski. Next, that advanced uphill ski is dragged on the snow at a slightly scissored-angle to the weight-bearing rear ski. It's like Snowshoe Thompson dragging his one ski pole on the side he wished to turn toward; only we drag a ski instead. The rear ski is edged uphill toward the turn as well, but much less so than the lead ski: just enough to be in position to carve on whatever side-cut it may have. The dragging lead ski helps the rear ski carve the turn, and on a smooth practice slope tracks can be studied to help learning along.

Solo Figure 8's

Independent Leg Action

After this simple, uphill scissors turn is mastered, we switch to untracked snow and a carving exercise I call solo figure eights. Down a gentle fall line, both knees and ski tips point out (bowlegged) until the skis carve out away from each other. Just before maximum straddle legging is achieved, both knees and tips reverse toward each other, knock-kneed, to carve the skis together again. Avoid pushing or pulling on the skis; let tip-pull, side-cut, and reverse camber do the work. Each ski's track should be no wider than the ski's shovel.

Figure-eights are just one way to play this carving exercise. If no fall line gentle enough is handy, let one ski go straight in some comfortable traverse, carrying most of the weight, while the unweighted ski carves out and away, then back in toward the straight tracking ski. It usually won't take the better students long before they start adding telemark stems and open scissors to these school figures, dramatically increasing turning power and decreasing the turning radius.

The scissors variation sees more daylight between knees than ankles. This seemingly awkward bowleggedness has the advantage in many types of layered or breakable snows. The lead ski breaks trail while lightly weighted, and the rear ski follows along behind, doing as much carving as conditions allow. Open ski tips, and the tendency of the skis to split apart from each other during crustal collapse, allows stepping and hopping recoveries with less chance of tangling skis. By contrast, conventional telemarks produce a knock-kneed leg configuration, and a tendency to cross skis when one layer collapses or runs faster than the other.

Many times, however, it is not the advantage of scissoring over stemming or vice versa that is most important. Rather, it is the necessity in tricky snow to maintain a telemark position as opposed to any particular style of turn. Once open turns are mastered, they can be alternated with conventional stemmed telemarks, leaving the same ski out in front until easier snow is reached. This ploy is known as the "Gunnar" around Kirkwood, California, after its most famous practitioner, Norwegian Gunnar Vadredt.

For crusts that break no matter how weight is distributed, various combinations of stepping, hopping, and even jumping, are traditional light nordic solutions to heavy snow problems. Airborn tactics, however, require the extra energy of take-off and landings, and are therefore avoided if possible on long tours. The telemark position, combined with either stemming or scissoring, is usually the most efficient solution which also maintains continuous snow contact.

Super steep and icy probably requires a better feel for maximum snow contact than any other kind of skiing. It is better to stem or scissor before any hopping here if possible. Stepping, however, is often an excellent way to maintain contact. Steve Barnett's description of turns being handed off from one ski to the other in stepped, open turns is an apt one.

Such turns often leave a set of off-set, parenthesis-like tracks down the hill, overlapping where one ski starts the next turn before the last ski finishes the previous. Many of these turns start as a stem telemark and end as a scissors telemark which requires only an edge change on the lead ski to carve into the next stem telemark. Much of the best alpine technique starts to generously overlap with cross-country downhill at this skill level. Independent leg action, avalement, anticipation, power or compression turns can be applied by alpine and nordic methods alike. The difference remains in the nordic substitution of a telemark position for the fore-and-aft stability of high boots. Which ski leads, or when, is much more flexible in nordic equipment, and learning to lead with either will make you a much more open and versatile telemarker.

Bumps/Moguls and Mental Attitude

Although considered 'sacreligious' by some cross-country ski purists, lift-serviced slopes can provide challenging conditions and thrilling terrain not often found in the backcountry. A steep, hard-packed mogul field, for example, may well rank as one of the most difficult and demanding testing grounds the total telemarker can face.

Even if you'd rather avoid them (and ski areas), altogether, bumps do exist in the backcountry, and chances are you'll run into them eventually.

More importantly, refining your skills in such conditions will definitely improve your overall telemark proficiency, no matter where you choose to ski.

Tom Carr (first nordic skier to descend Mexico's 18,700-foot Pico de Orizaba), is one of the best bump technicians today, as well as a superior all around skier. I think you'll find his advice on moguls invaluable to every telemark situation you may encounter.

> *More than anything else, the key to mogul skiing is a matter of mental attitude: you've got to be psyched for them from the start or they'll knock you down -- fast. They require total concentration at all times, and lightning reflexes: a quick mind coupled with quick feet.*
> *I ski moguls on nordic gear just as I do on alpine: although the methods*

of technique may differ, the approach is the same.

I try to stay right in the fall line, relying on short radius turns straight down. Rather than following the path between, or on top of, the bumps, I turn where I want to. If there's a bump ahead, I use my knees to absorb it instead of changing my direction to avoid it.

My weight shifts are very fast; although I'm generally centered, 90% of my mass is over my front ski during the initiation of the turn, and my back ski doesn't stay back there long.

There is no room for hesitation, or wavering between turns. I just change my leads, touch both feet and go. When I make a mistake -- when I fail to turn immediately after I change leads -- I find it is often more effective to use a Gunnar turn than to disrupt my rhythm by attempting to change leads in midstride. I just keep my feet where they are and turn with the 'wrong' ski forward, then go immediately into a new lead and turn.

As soon as I know I have lost the rhythm, or am not in the right frame of mind, I'll stop and take time to think -- to focus -- before going on again.

Quick mind, quick reactions and quick feet are the keys to bump telemarking.

The super steep of Orizaba's summit/*Mike Carr Photo*

The "Para-Tele," or "Parallel-a-Mark"

As it's nickname(s) suggest, the "para-tele" is a hybrid, combining the advanced turning principles of modern alpine technique with the basic stability of a modified telemark form. It is almost a pure parallel, except for the position of the feet during the phase between turns. They are spread apart fore and aft in a modified telemark stance, with the downhill ski advanced -- in contrast to a parallel traverse position. Also, the center of gravity is held higher, and the base narrower, than in a classic telemark.

The result is a highly refined form of nordic downhill technique, although a highly specialized one as well. It is very effective in certain conditions -- such as groomed, hard-packed slopes -- but works best if you use the right kind of equipment. Don't try this one on light touring skis without sidecut, or in tricky snow on any type of gear.

Rather than relying on the arcing nature of two skis angled together -- as in the classic telemark approach -- the "para-tele" utilizes the inherent carving characteristics of today's alpine-style, nordic downhill ski designs, which enable each ski to turn independently of the other.

Without the supplemental support of a locked-heel binding system, however, nordic technique still relies on some form of the telemark stance for stability, and the "para-tele" is no exception.

The turn is executed as a parallel by changing edges and applying pressure on the uphill ski, with most of your weight forward and feet side by side. As the turn is finished, however, the downhill ski moves ahead, and your center of mass shifts down and back into a modified telemark stance once again.

Powder: The Breakfast of Champions

In the hierarchy of super skiing, powder snow is considered magical territory, a sacred realm reached by a special quest. For many it offers the sport's quintessential experience: an ultimate, spiritual encounter on skis.

True powder is loose, light and dry, falls mainly in high, cold ranges and usually stays purest on northern slopes, where the mid-winter sun never shines. For avid powder hounds -- nordic or alpine -- such snow can never be deep enough. When it is billowing over your head, though -- splashing 'cold smoke' in your face and blocking your airway -- it's bordering on perfection. Sensual, serene, energizing and ecstatic, linking telemark turns through powder can indeed be like Nirvana on earth.

It can also be frustrating as hell if you don't know what you're doing, and sometimes just getting down the mountain can be a real challenge when you're wet, cold and exhausted. At first, you'll probably spend more time digging yourself out after countless falls than actually skiing, and your tracks will look more like random bomb-craters than anything else.

If you survive your introduction to deep powder snow, chances are you'll be ready for more. Let your muscles and pride recover on old familiar terrain, get your confidence and Ski to Die attitude back, wait for the next big dump, wax 'em up and go for greatness. In time you'll find the telemark turn in deep snow is amazingly simple, and once you link two good turns together, you'll be hooked forever.

You can find good powder at lift-serviced areas, or right next to the packed touring track. The 'rush,' or pleasure-factor, can be the same in both radical and novice terrain, and your last tracks can be as sensational as your first. Even the devout wilderness tourer has to admit that when the backcountry is too deep and dangerous for travel, the turns never end at controlled ski areas. When you consider, too, the sheer number of runs made possible by riding lifts, practicing telemark turns at a ski area can be well worth the price of a day ticket. As Lito Tejada-Flores says in his excellent book, **Back-Country Skiing**: "Powder is where you find it."

Remember, though, that area skiing is limited by definition to certain boundaries, and those boundaries are meant to be inviolable. Respect them! When you purchase a lift ticket, make the most of it, but stay within the designated terrain. Sure it's tough, when the only thing separating you from what appears to be a perfectly good powder run is a bright orange strand of marker-rope, and a Forest Service sign. Though you probably won't get hurt, or lost, or caught (in which cases you could die or face stiff penalties), what's the point? Cross-country telemark skiing allows you to go anywhere else you want -- where the only

Doug Buzzell buried/*Colorado First Tracks* Photo

Craig Hall/Co. First Tracks Photo

boundary is your own expertise, and your only responsibility is to yourself and your companions. Save your out-of-bounds skiing for the backcountry, where it belongs.

Good powder skiers, especially telemarkers, almost seem to float. Their movements are so smooth and fluid, rhythmic and relaxed that they actually become one with the snow -- a part of the flow.

The trick is simple: keep your weight over both skis and your motions as subtle as possible. You'll quickly learn that the slightest change in body position will initiate a turn in powder, and as soon as you move too far forward, back, or to the sides, the snow will grab your skis and send you flying.

While your stance should generally be centered, you'll find you really have to concentrate on weighting the back foot more than the front in order to achieve equal distribution. If your rear ski tends to drift out from beneath you, or crosses behind the lead ski, press harder and get down over that rear foot. Don't lean back with your upper body, but drop your hips instead.

Telemark Shuffle in Powder

To make lead changes smoothly, try unweighting your skis with a simple 'sucking-up' action in your legs -- instead of an exaggerated raising of your upper body, or emphatic step forward. Think of yourself as a cat slinking down stairs: your head, shoulders and torso travel along constant planes, while your legs act like shock absorbers underneath.

To initiate a turn, unweight in the same way.

Release pressure on your feet by drawing your knees up. As the skis come off their edges, they will tend to jet ahead, with the tips planing above the snow. Follow this jetting action by smoothly extending and pointing with your front foot. Press gently to the inside with your knees and edge slightly with both ankles.

When skiing waist-deep powder in open bowls or broad meadows, you'll experience both bouyancy and resistance. You'll find yourself suspended above the ground, flowing freely within an almost liquid-like element, yet surrounded by enough friction to moderate the forces of gravity and enough resiliency beneath the foot to provide an impulse for unweighting. In other words, you can point your skis downhill, step from foot to foot like a cat and stay right in the fall line without worrying about going too fast.

Check Telemark in Powder

Powder skiing in tree-lined chutes or narrow couloirs, though, requires a tighter series of turns. You'll want to let your skis swing further around the slope, with greater emphasis on steering, edging and up-down motion during each turn. Instead of shuffling straight down the fall line with almost parallel lead-changes, increase hip-swivel and counter-rotation. Point your forward-moving ski more positively in the new direction, and complete each turn with a vigorous edge-set. Drive around the fall line with your knees and feet until your skis are perpendicular to the slope, sink and twist downhill with your hips over both skis and weight your tails to establish a definite platform. *Change leads, steer, compress, check, and rebound.* Always keep an anticipating upper body position, and use a degree of angulation that is con-commitant to the degree of the slope, conditions of snow, speed and radius of turn required. Generally, in deep powder you don't have to angulate much, unles you want to check, rebound and short-swing.

Spring and Summer Corn

Long after most lift-serviced areas have closed, when many winter fanatics have hung up their touring boots in favor of beach sandals, a whole new ski season begins in the high country -- just waiting to be discovered.

Above lush meadows, bursting with flowers and cascading waterfalls, upper basins hold their snow well into May, June, or July. Areas of the Rockies, Sierras, North Cascades, White Mountains and other ranges open up which during winter require major expeditions to reach. That peak you saw from the chairlift -- far away across endless snowfields -- can be driven to, climbed and descended in a single day.

When you hit it right, and the upper layers of snow have softened but the pack remains firm underneath, you can carve smooth, fluid turns on the most radical terrain you can find. Your skis will hold with a minimum amount of effort. With good edges, you can check-telemark, step-or-stem down steep faces, bank and loop your way through rolling bowls, and parallel or gorilla-hop through narrow couloirs.

Spring snow can be tricky, though, and conditions can change drastically in a matter of minutes. The slightest variation in temperature may alter the snowpack, suddenly leaving you with a scary descent.

The most important thing to learn about corn snow telemarking then, is not so much *how* to ski it but *when* to ski it. For snow to reach the ideal corn stage it must go through a definite cycle of melting and refreezing.

Depending on the location and particular weather of your environment, the spring snowpack is best at different times and stays longer on different exposures. In general, though, look for the corn to appear first on the southern and southeastern slopes, where fluxuations in temperature between day and night are most extreme.

Since the amount of free water flowing down and weakening the lower layers reaches a peak between 1:00 and 4:00 pm, an early start is essential.

Penelope Street's perfect poise/ *Rick Borkovec Photo*

FREE-STYLE JUMPING

Axel Henriksen somersaulting in Duluth, Minn., 1913

Tommy "Crash" Craddock in backward somersault

Three-pin jumper/*D. Pierson Photo*

Tom Carr sideways/*J. Kahnweiler Photo*

In 1982, at Aspen, Co., Keith Calhoun of Crested Butte and Katie Pytell of Winter Park became the first North American Telemark Slalom Champions ever crowned/*B. English Photo*

For sheer drama and color, perhaps the greatest race ever held in Colorado took place at Crested Butte on Washington's Birthday, February 22, 1886.

As word of the event spread, the first in a competitive circuit established by the Gunnison County Snowshoe Club that same year, the best skiers from eight surrounding towns gathered in Crested Butte for a chance to win a $20.00 first prize -- more than any miner could make in a week.

The course was set on a hill just south of town and measured 525-yards. The racers would dash down a thirty-five degree slope, and many undoubtedly took deep gulps when their eyes gazed upon what they had to come down. When they hit the bottom of the hill, they would have another 250-feet of flat ground before they passed through the finish. With an estimated 1,000 screaming spectators lining the course, Charlie Baney of Crested Butte (age 16), Al Johnson and Al Fish of Crystal, and Harry Cornwall of Irwin each won two heats in a row to qualify for the finals.

Picture, if you will, the great drama unfolding on that winter day in 1886 as Baney, Johnson, Fish and Cornwall -- their muscles tightening, the tension building in their faces -- prepared to race more than a quarter of a mile at break-neck speeds for the glory of their town, the accolades of their friends and the title of "Champion Skier of the Rocky Mountains."

A rifle shot was the signal to start, and with its report, all four "shot down the deep declivity like bullet(s) through the air." Baney and Johnson immediately gained the lead. At the quarter mark, Baney, "the light, nimble little fellow," pulled ahead.

Time after time, Johnson made valiant attempts to overtake the youngster, and twice managed to pass him. But Baney, catching a glimpse of the mail-carrier from Crystal, "would lower his guide pole, double himself on his shoes until he seemed only a small ball and would instantly shoot forward again." When the two men crossed the finish line at better than sixty-five miles per hour, it was Baney in the lead by a scant two-feet.

Of the sixteen competitors, only two had been injured: George Hale had broken his leg and George Cornwall suffered a severe sprain of his left ankle.

The next day, most of the rugged competitors skied back to their respective jobs in the various towns of the Gunnison Country.

Dr. Duane Vandenbusche
"The Great Snowshoer
of the Gunnison Country"

Lateral projection in the gates/*Eric Sanford Photo*

V TELEMARK RACING

Crested Butte, Colorado: March 17, 1977. *The dual slalom downhill race held Sunday afternoon during Crested Butte's annual Nordic Fest proved to be an exciting format for telemark competition...and demonstrated once again the extent to which local cross-country skiers are advancing the state of the art (and) redefining the sport of touring...in a competition that will sweep the nation and perhaps the world in the coming years.*

Brad English
for the **Crested Butte Pilot**

The great French alpine ski technician, Georges Joubert, points out the fundamental interrelationship between racing and recreational skiing:

> The art of skiing resides in the sliding of the skis -- what in France we call glissement...the latest discoveries of today's (racing) champions marks a sharp improvement in the technique of sliding and carving the skis. This fact is of more than normal interest to the recreational skier because it is a technique applicable to all kinds of terrain and snow.[1]

So it is with today's telemark slalom racing technique. Always looking for the smoothest, most direct and therefore fastest line possible, champions on the North American Telemark circuit have refined their forms to absolute essentials, increasing efficiency through simplification. Yet their turns must still be initiated by the telemark technique, thus maintaining a nordic approach.

Even if your favorite 'course' is a powder chute through the trees, running gates on free-

Concentration/J. Kahnweiler Photo

heeled nordic equipment will teach you fundamental techniques which are applicable to almost any cross-country downhill situation.

More often than not, the best skiers on the race course are outstanding all around skiers as well. So, whether you want to race competitively or not, slalom training is an important part of total telemarking. It's fun, it's informative, and if you **are** competitive by nature, slalom racing is an exciting and challenging format for telemark skiing.

Keith Calhoun offers a few suggestions for beginning telemark slalom training:

Course Analysis

"Racers ready! Set! Three...Two...One...Go!" The cadence of the starter's countdown suggests the tempo and timing of the turns to come: the rhythm of the run.

Study the rhythm of the course, noting gates which create a change in the rhythm: long turns to short turns, and short to long turns. The last gate before a transition indicates how to set up your approach to the first gate of the transition.

Julie Neils demonstrates a racing start/N. Bilow Photos

Memorize visual clues, like outstanding terrain characteristics beside the course, which indicate upcoming changes one or two gates in advance, to allow enough time to set up.

Observe snow conditions between gates, especially ice, fresh snow, and places where fresh snow changes to icy conditions or deep ruts.

Note problem gates. Off-set gates which change rhythm and fall away gates on top of a knoll in icy conditions can be particularly tricky. So can the finish gate. Many veterans put in a great run only to fall at the last. You want to maintain the forward momentum of body and mind without being too eager or breaking your concentration before crossing the finish line.

The Start

Extend forward without bending at the waist.

Keep your head up, and your eyes looking down the course.

Push off your poles, and continue backward thrust until hands are behind your hips.

Telemark racing technique/*Paul Gallaher Photos*

Maintaining a Winning Line

The fastest way through a set of gates is the straightest, most direct line, with the least amount of turns and maximum amount of sliding. But smoothness is also essential, since you can't go perfectly straight. You must turn, and turn at the right time.

Don't be late. Make your turn at the earliest possible time and most efficient manner possible to achieve the straightest line as you pass the gate.

Set up early. Initiate your turns emphatically, employing anticipation and angulation as needed, and then let your skis run. "Edge set and rebound! Edge set and rebound. This is the way to go fast!" says Murray Cunningham, one of the founders of Phoenix Skis and one of the top ten racers at the 1982 North American Telemark Championships.

The first telemark slalom was staged in 1974 by Gene Dayton at the Return of the Telemark festival in Breckenridge. In 1979, three young Summit County skiers, Bob Curfman, Ken Emrick, and Art Burrows organized the tour-race Summit Telemark Series.

Each year the Series has expanded and the competition grown keener as more and more skiers, from beginners to experienced Olympians have taken to freeheeling on the slopes and in the backcountry. The Summit Series is their meeting ground for having fun and improving technique and provides a real test for manufacturers trying to keep up with the skiers' demands.

The Uphill, Downhill, All-Terrain Telemark Race

The most demanding format for telemark competition combines the diverse challenges of several different nordic events together in a single race. Such a course incorporates the extended distances and varying terrain of cross-country running, the open-field navigation of ski-orienteering, the precision descents of telemark slalom, the wide-radius high-speed turns of alpine giant slalom and downhill, and the untracked conditions of backcountry touring. None has yet included the flight-time of a 90-meter nordic ramp, nor the gelandesprung bump of a professional head-to-head alpine slalom format.

All things considered, though, the 'uphill, downhill, all-terrain' ski race course separates the men and women from the boys and girls as far as total telemarking is concerned.

The Al Johnson Memorial Race

Doug Buzzell originally organized this mass-start, cross-country, uphill/downhill race as part of the 1974 Crested Butte NordicFest. It is perhaps the purest challenge of all around skiing skill: 'There is simply a mountain to be skied.'

The only rules are that free-heeled nordic equipment must be used, and competitors must cross the finish line wearing all their gear.

The course on Crested Butte Mountain Resort's North Face begins with a mass start of

The mass start of the Al Johnson Memorial/N. Bilow Photo

all competitors: a Geschmozzel (German for, 'mass free-for-all'). This is Gate #1.

It continues with a gruelling climb to The Notch, consisting of moderate, rolling terrain; a traverse and then a steady ascent to the saddle. This section tests wax, as well as demands pace and stamina. You don't want to burn out here; save some juice for the descent.

All skiers must pass through The Notch (high point), where they can view Johnson's mail route in the distance. But they have no time for scenery. This is Gate #2, and from here it is wide open and all downhill.

The descent of the North Face plunges 1200 vertical feet over three pitches from 35-45 degrees in steepness, and conditions may range from untracked powder to crude, from ruts to hardpacked alpine moguls.

The final pitch is the steepest and narrowest, and a single mistake here can cost the leader victory. In addition to the radical terrain, hazards include the fallen bodies and strewn equipment of other competitors.

The finish is always closely fought, ending with an abrupt compression and flat runout.

Craig Hall holds the record time of 5 minutes, 53 seconds.

"When conditions are unstable, the wise travel only for the rescue of fools."

Ron Perla

The frozen silence of a deep winter's dawn is suddenly shattered by the approaching sound of a Chinook helicopter -- the distinctive "whock-whock" of her massive twin engines amplified by the peaks surrounding the airport where we wait. Immediately, the apprehension felt by each member of the rescue team is replaced by the familiar rush of adrenaline which always seems to accompany this sound. For us, it signals a call to action: after hours of futile immobility and frustrated helplessness, the beginning of the mission means the first real opportunity for success. For the lone skier we seek, it signals perhaps the last remaining hope of survival...if only he is still alive to hear it.

Despite the confidence the arrival of this awesome mercy ship brings, the situation is grim, and an overwhelming sense of despair is unmistakable in our faces as we prepare to board and lift off.

Since the lost skier's departure from town one week ago -- headed out on a solo cross-country trip to Aspen that was supposed to take three days at most -- more than 110 inches of new snow had fallen, and temperatures had reached -40°F. Despite national weather forecasts which accurately predicted the impending storm, and the vehement objections of more knowledgeable friends, he not only chose the worst possible time for his tour but followed the most dangerous route as well.

Covering 35 miles of remote wilderness by way of an 11,000 foot pass, the trail he attempted crosses numerous avalanche zones which are hazardous in the best of conditions. Looking down from the helicopter at the terrain below, straining to catch a glimpse of his ski-tracks or sign of his camp, we see only the tree-shattered debris of massive snow slides on all exposures. Everything which could have run already has, and it's clear there's been enough subsequent snowfall to cause everything to slide again. Beyond the avalanche problem, chest-deep snow, poor visibility and paralyzing cold have combined to create conditions severe enough to challenge the strongest, most experienced party of skiers.

But the skier we seek is alone, and judging by the description we have from those who watched him go (in spite of all their attempts to dissuade him), he is neither strong nor experienced.

Had he been knowledgeable in avalanche and survival skills, he might have been able to avoid the major slide paths and establish a secure camp. With warm clothing, bivouac gear, food, water and luck, he might have been able to endure the storm. And while no one who ventures into the backcountry can ever depend on the rescue efforts of others in times of emergency, had he done things differently, he might have lived to tell about the time he was evacuated in the world's largest ski lift: the Chinook helicopter.

But he had taken none of the precautions or equipment which might have changed the outcome.

★ He wore bluejean slacks, and carried no change of clothing.

★ He wore lightweight, unlined touring boots, totally unsuited for sub-zero temperatures or rugged mountain terrain.

★ He was completely unfamiliar with his chosen route, and the nature of its hazards.

★ He took a map, but no compass.

★ He had no stove, and carried only carrots and walnuts for nourishment. (Have you ever tried to eat a carrot at 40° below zero?).

★ He carried a summer-weight sleeping bag and a plastic tube tent.

★ He had no shovel, no tools, no spare parts, no first aid.

★ He was a novice skier.

In short, he broke all the standard rules of backcountry safety, and ignored the obvious warning signs which all pointed to extreme and immediate danger. As a result, he would pay the ultimate price.

Outward vision is obscured by great funnels of powder snow swirling up from surrounding slopes to envelope us; the low-hanging clouds and high winds continually beat us back from the high mountain ridge. As the rocking helicopter circles, probing for a way over, a passenger inside spots something in the snow below.

"There, just short of the pass! A Forest Service cabin, and fresh ski tracks! And there! Aren't those more signs of life?" he asks over his headset. It's hard to tell; not everyone has a clear view. What little I can make out isn't very reassuring. The apparent camp lies on the side of a narrow drainage. Above it loom steep slide-paths. Deep snow obscures all terrain directly below the ship, and our only landing zone is uncertain at best.

It becomes more and more difficult to see out the windows; this and the overwhelming reverberating noise in the chopper's massive hull combine to cause an almost complete loss of orientation. But as I look across the hold at my teammate, Craig Hall, whose eyes suddenly widen within his goggles, whose knuckles clench more tightly to his seat, I sense we and the ship are going down and fast. Craig had experienced a previous crash landing in another wilderness emergency. What I only sensed now, he knew. Then, an abrupt jolt throws me against my seat harness; the craft's wild lurch is followed by the sickening groan of twisting metal. There is a pause. The ship, her front rotor blades whirling only 12 feet above the ground, begins to slide sideways down the drainage slope. Another pause...the one that seems to last an eternity. Then the helicopter lifts her nose into the air, floats up and back, hangs momentarily and wheels around aloft in one smooth surge of power to finally face down-valley and regain controlled flight.

It was not until we made a forced landing in Aspen just before dark that we learned what actually happened in those few moments. As the Chinook had settled her rear wheels in that narrow draw and brought her front wheels down, she had struck a boulder buried just beneath the snow -- torqueing the right-forward landing strut 90 degrees to the side. Only the quick judgement and decisive actions of the pilot had saved the craft from augering in and self-destructing in a mass of whirling steel and crew members as the rotor blades struck the earth.

It was not until the following August -- when a summer hiking party came upon a pair of grisly feet emerging from the gradually receding snowpack -- that the Crested Butte Search and Rescue Team could return to retrieve the remains of this poor soul whose mistake had almost cost us our lives as well as his own.

Mexico's Popocatepetl/M. Carr Photo

VI SKI MOUNTAINEERING
THE CREME de la CREME

Backcountry, by the very nature of its isolation, remains a land of enchantment. It intrigues to the degree that it becomes land inaccessible, and thus to the degree that it is unspoiled...

Calvin Rustrum, **Backcountry**

In the beginning there was snow, and everywhere -- but for a few small clusters -- was backcountry. Ever since the first skier/explorer penetrated the heart of wilderness' icy nature, others have continually pushed back the boundaries of the inaccessible, and conquered what was once remote, or unknown. Whether or not it is thus spoiled, and without intrigue -- as Rustrum suggests -- what little backcountry there is retains its essential wildness in unchangeable ways. The awe it still inspires in us is equal only to the destruction it can inflict, and anyone who ventures into the special realm of winter would do well to tread lightly indeed.

Skiing the backcountry safely is much more involved than the simple act of gliding over snow. The elements you face are merciless, constantly changing and beyond ultimate human control. Without the security of immediate assistance, everything you do acquires added significance, and there is little room for error. Simple mistakes -- not necessarily in technique -- have a way of triggering a chain of circumstances which can lead inexhorably to disaster. An easy fall head-first into a tree-well, a missed turn in a white-out, a forced bivouac in sub-zero temperature, broken bindings, wet clothes, exhaustion, minor injuries, the careless actions of others or the whims of nature can suddenly place an entire ski party in a life-or-death situation. You better be ready, and you better know what to do.

Arm thyself with knowledge, then, and learn

in advance as much as you can about the nature of the backcountry, the related skills you'll need and the tools you'll want to meet the challenge of its harsh terms with confidence. Advanced touring requires familiarity with snow science, hazard evaluation, weather forecasting, routefinding, map and compass, winter camping, wilderness survival, equipment repair, emergency medical assistance and mountain rescue procedures. With adequate training, thorough planning, proper gear, sound judgment, close attention to potential danger, and appropriate response capabilities, most accidents can be avoided or minimized.

In addition to extensive literary research and independent study, beginning with the bibliography at this chapter's end, I highly recommend you enroll in one of the numerous snow safety courses taught by experienced professional instructors around the country. The American Avalanche Institute, for example, offers a wide-ranging curriculum of excellent seminars at several different U.S. locales. Combining classroom theory with practical field application in varying degrees of duration and intensity, the Institute and its instructors provide a solid, workable insight into the essential aspects of snow-related safety for recreational and professional skiers alike.

Other U.S. organizations, like the National Ski Patrol System and local search and rescue groups, also play a valuable role in the education of the skiing public -- as well as provide voluntary life-saving assistance in times of emergency. Make as much use as you can of the expertise of such services and the willingness of their members to teach you all they know about safe skiing.

Eric Burr -- renowned ski-mountaineering guide, wilderness ranger, and driving force behind the formation of a Nordic Patrol within the National Ski Patrol System -- keenly analyzes backcountry skiing's current problems in this contribution, entitled:

Where is the Nordic Patrol?

Ninety pounds of rucksack, a pound of grub or two, and he'll schuss the mountains like his daddy used to do.

So goes the chorus of a traditional ski patrol song hinting at proud and liftless beginnings. Now, however, most skiers associate the ski patrol entirely with lifts.

Yet, as nordic skiing matures, it is inevitable that greater numbers of skiers will put themselves at risk by pushing whatever limits of the sport happen to intrigue them. While cross-country skiing's enviable reputation of relative safety has recently been called into question by an embarrassing rise in search-and-rescue incidents, as well as avalanche fatalities, the accident rate is low enough that many skiers ignore the early warning signs. The time to worry about skiing safety is **now**, before enough fatalities make headlines to arouse the general public, and restrict our sport's freedom.

The responsible nordic skier can prevent and prepare for possible emergencies in many ways. First, find out what kinds of nordic patrols are operating where you ski, and know how to contact them in an emergency. Get their advice on the situations peculiar to your locale. Listen to their opinion of your chosen route, and their predictions of the conditions you'll likely encounter. File a written 'flight plan' with the patrol which details the nature of your trip: date of departure, intended route, names of members, their closest relatives, friends at start and finish, estimated time of arrival, and any other information which might be needed in case of emergency. Secondly, you can learn about snow safety on your own, and personally assess the potential hazards of proposed ski tours to increase your individual security. Third, if you encounter skiers endangering themselves or others, don't hesitate to provide a friendly word of warning. You may wind up hauling them out! And finally, you can help nordic patrolling, and everyone's skiing safety, by referring others to safety information made available by professionals who care.

Also recommended is a course in first aid, such as the Advanced Red Cross or Emergency Medical Technician programs. A thorough knowledge of emergency care may come in handy in everyday situations; in a backcountry crisis, where the risk of injury and lack of immediate professional assistance is greatest, your educated medical actions may well make the difference between life and death. Carry a full medical kit whenever you ski, and know how to use its contents.

Of course, nothing can take the place of personal experience, but you have to survive long enough in order to gain it. While neither classrooms nor book learning will teach you all you need to know about the potential situations you may encounter, by practicing the simple guidelines offered here and in more thorough references, you will definitely increase your chances of skiing the backcountry safely time after time.

This, after all, is the meaning of the total telemarker's credo: *"Live to ski, ski to die, and live to ski another day."*

The Backcountry Telemarker's Playground

Snow is the *raison d'etre* of skiing. Without snow there would be no way to reduce friction and generate momentum, temper speed and change direction, flow with gravity down the face of a mountain or glide along the level land, yet no matter how good a skier you are, familiarity with snow cannot be taken for granted. There's more to be aware of, more to be considered, than what happens on its surface.

Picture a range of lofty peaks blanketed in white, serene against the azure sky. The day is very calm, and everywhere there is silence. From high up on the faces, great spouts of ice issue forth, frozen in time. Except for the red-tailed hawk wheeling around the summits, there seems no motion.

In truth the snowfield is never at rest. Its molecules are all dancing around in a very excited state, susceptible to rapid and irratic change. It settles, creeps and glides along right beneath your skis, pulled by gravity. According to Reinhold Messner, the Khumbu Ice Fall at the base of Mt. Everest, for example, moves at the rate of one meter per day, but you'd never know it by looking at it.

Peter Lev, an outstanding 'field researcher' in avalanche phenomenon (and instructor with the American Avalanche Institute) once advised me to think of a slope of snow as a carpet hung on the wall, always wanting to slide down to the floor where it belongs. Like a wave of ice paused at its crest, it can crash at any moment.

Because of its unstable nature, snow is always building up potential energy in the form of stress. Although its plastic qualities give it a certain amount of elasticity, snow is also brittle and prone to catastrophic failure. When a steep enough slope becomes critically loaded, the release of its tension can be abrupt and dramatic. The result is often an avalanche, and its power is awesome.

Reaching speeds in excess of 200 miles per hour, the largest snow slides have a maximum force of impact great enough to move a steel-reinforced concrete structure. Even more typical, a dry snow avalanche may contain sufficient power to uproot mature trees.

The **Avalanche Handbook** describes the grim details of a "white death":

> Although avalanches kill people in many ways, the great majority of fatalities are due to suffocation... The weight of snow bears down on the victim's throat and chest...so tightly that the victim is immobilized and must helplessly await his fate.
>
> Some victims are killed outright...dashed into a tree...or hit by flying debris. Head injuries, abdominal injuries, and broken necks, backs and legs are common...Some victims die of hypothermia, exhaustion, or shock. Less than 20% of the victims buried with no trace showing are recovered alive.

This last statistic is particularly revealing: Even people who are uninjured, conscious and breathing face almost certain death if completely buried. It only takes enough snow to cover a person in order to kill them, and the horrible truth is that most avalanche fatalities result from small slides (those that travel less than 100 meters).

Thus, to ski the backcountry -- where most avalanche accidents occur -- is to risk its inherent dangers. Those who choose to ski it anyway willingly accept responsibility for the potential consequences their decision implies. The name of the game, then, is to keep the odds on your side. Since the stakes are always the same -- your life -- and the deck is stacked against you, your best bet is to play it safe. You win by never losing, but once you're beaten, you're out of the game...for keeps!

Stability Evaluation & Hazard Forecasting

To improve overall safety and reduce the odds of snow burial as much as possible, the backcountry skier should be able to recognize the factors of terrain, snow, and weather which spell high avalanche danger in general, and determine in advance the relative likelihood of actual avalanche occurence given the conditions of the moment.

From the scientific evaluation of current data, the speculation of future trends, and the cosmic magic of intuitive feeling, the semi-informed skier can make a rough guess as to whether or not the game is worth the risk.

Avalanche forecasting -- judging when and where avalanches are most likely to occur -- is a rough, young science at best. The 'experts' who ought to know maintain, "the only rule of thumb, when it comes to avalanches, is: there is no rule of thumb." It's probably safe to suggest, though, that another rule is to avoid any area where snow instability is even remotely suspected.

Avalanche Hazard Evaluation Factors

1. Past observed weather and snowpack conditions. (Know how stable pack was prior to new storm and what changes may effect it).

2. Past observed avalanche activity.

3. Current local meteorological data.
   a. Air temperature
   b. Wind
   c. Humidity
   d. Bp.
   e. Snowfall intensity
   f. Precipitation intensity
   g. New grain type
   h. Total accumulation

4. U.S. Weather forecasts

5. Current observed avalanche activity

6. Snowpit analysis: provides preliminary forecast data.

7. On-slope testing (ski-cutting, explosive control): confirms or alters forecast.

Look, listen, learn and live: a lesson in avalanche awareness/*Eric Burr Illustration*

TOOLS FOR THE TELEMARKER

THE DAY-TOURER's OVERNIGHT PACK

As Murphy's Law so aptly states: 'If something *can* go wrong, it *will*!' When something goes wrong in the winter backcountry, even the casual day tour may become a frightening -- or potentially fatal -- ordeal. If help is further away than crawling distance, the emergency gear you carry on your own back can mean the difference between life and death.

Chances are you'll never need half the items you should bring along, but ultimately what matters is having them all that one time when **you need them more than anything else in the world.**

Here's what professional ski guides and winter mountaineers commonly recommend as the basic contents of a backcountry ski touring pack. With these few essentials, you stand a good chance of avoiding, or at least surviving, the first 24-48 hours of a winter emergency:

1. Maps and Compass
2. Fire and Fuel
   - waterproof matches, lighter, flint and steel, etc.
   - candles
   - flammable material (eg., toilet paper, rag soaked in wax-remover solution, etc.)
3. Medical
   - standard bandages, compresses, lots of wide, waterproof adhesive tape, gauze rolls and pads
   - large triangular bandages
   - iodine, antiseptic cream, sunscreen lotion, lip balm
   - mole skin (for blisters)
   - scissors, knife, tweezers
   - needles and thread (dental floss works

well as thread for almost all sewing jobs)
- salt tabs, sucrose, aspirin, vitamins, etc.
- tongue depressors, splint material
- oral-pharyngial airway (optional)

4. Food and Drink
   - (Remember: unless you have a good supply of burnable calories in your stomach, no amount of clothing will keep you warm for long. Also, avoid dehydration.)
   - canteen of water
   - tea, bullion cubes, instant beverage mix, electrolyte drink, etc.
   - energy bars, fruit, chocolate, etc.
   - container with lid in which to heat liquids

5. Equipment Repair Kit
   - (Remember, without a properly functioning system of skis, boots and bindings, travel in deep snow is virtually impossible. Two whole, stout ski poles with baskets also help.)
   - handyman tool: pliers, phillip's-head and regular screwdriver all-in-one
   - extra screws, nuts, bolts
   - duct tape, baling wire, accessory straps, webbing, boot laces, steel wool
   - extra ski pole basket and ski tip
   - two aluminum tent stakes of the half-curve type to splint broken ski pole shaft
   - spare batteries, bulbs, boot laces, etc.

6. Rescue and Survival
   - space blankets (lightweight/compact, and duo-layered, quilted/tarp varieties should both be carried)
   - flashlight -- preferably a head-lamp type
   - signal whistle, mirror or shiny metal wax scraper
   - snow shovel
   - recycled piece of old ensolite pad, large enough to sit and stand on
   - bivvy sac (optional)
   - makeshift sled system improvised with skis, poles, internal pack stays, tape, rope and whatever works for emergency transport (optional)

7. Extra Clothing
   - spare wool hat, mittens, socks
   - scarf or face mask
   - foul-weather suit
   - down vest, wool sweater, pile liner, polarguard jacket or other garment that is warm when wet and easily dried

(Remember, hypothermia is most common when temperatures are above freezing. In essence, most victims 'chill to death' because the dampness of the air causes 200-times faster heat loss vs. dry air conditions. Greatest heat-loss always occurs from the head. As the Eskimoes say, "When your feet are cold, put on your hat.")

I. Snow Crystal Characteristics/ Snowpack Structures

A. Constantly changing, dynamic mass of ice grains, whose properties include: viscosity, brittleness, instability, and stored potential energy. Different grains have different textures/feeling, depending upon the nature of the pack. These textures are meaningful indicators of the stability of a slope.

B. Original crystal-form identification is not as important as changed (metamorphosed), grain identification. This type is the primary concern of avalanche study.

C. Mechanisms causing transformation:
1. Molecular heat exchange W — C (warm to cold
   a. Between air and snow surface: wind shear always warms surface.
   b. Surface radiation/absorbtion depends on length of day, cloud cover, slope aspect, snow's water equivalent. Dry, new snow reflects 90% shortwave/wet snow absorbs 50%
   c. Within snow layers: differences in temperature of 1° Cel./10 cm. creates **temperature gradient** that drives heat transfer between layers.
2. Temperature gradient (TG) metamorphism:
   a. bonded grains enlarge at expense of interconnecting necks, producing coarse, separated, angular, plated grains and cohesionless, weak snowpack

Beginning-to-intermediate stages of TG crystals in average pack, indicating a potential weak layer or sliding surface when found at bed surface or within pack. Advanced TG is especially common in thin, old/early-season snowpacks. Depth Hoar (adv. TG at bed layer), in excess of 8 inches is hazardous.

3. Equi-Temperature (ET) met-amorphism: a process of simplification which results in a natural settling/adjustment of newly fallen grains. Grains become:
   a. More rounded/simpler
   b. Interconnected by small **necks** of ice
   c. well-bonded/cohesive/strong
4. Melt-Freeze (MF) met: caused by drastically fluctuating temps. during 24-hour period.
   a. Warmer/wetter surface absorbs 40% more solar radiation
   b. Resulting free water from melted upper grains percolates down through pack, flowing horizontally along dense layers and eroding interfaces above and below
   c. Forms large clusters of very small (smaller than ET), angular grains.
   d. Bonds are eroded and layers of Advanced TG are melted first.
5. Graupel, Sleet and Hail/Riming: Colliding snow crystals are coated with frozen, super-cooled water droplets
   a. Usually associated with cold front, when turbulence is highest
   b. Graupel (heaviest riming type) indicates passage of cold front
   c. Easily seen in snowpit as loose, styrofoam-type like balls
   d. Most important modified grain-type: resulting instability 'primarily' confined to slab releases of one storm's thickness.

II. Meteorological Factors

In addition to the mechanisms of temperature, other changes on or within the snowpack are caused by weather -- the second aspect of the backcountry environment. Air temperature, aside major effects of meteorological factors include:

A. **Wind Flow** over mountain terrain has immense impact on nature of snowpack. Airspeed accelerates in updraft on windward slope, reaches maximum velocity at ridge crest, and decelerates on leeward side.
   1. Wind-transportation of snow results in scouring/hardening on windward: drifting/cornicing on lee.
   2. Windspeed in excess of 5 m/s required for lee-slope loading. Loaded zone = avalanche zone
   3. Wind pulverizes grains and reduces their size by 90%.
   4. These densified grains cause hard, slab-like pack: very compact, and unstable. Indicated by stiffer texture/propogation of either small cracks or large, definite fractures. Anytime the slightest crack appears in front of your ski tips, a slab-formation is present, suggesting avalanche hazard.
   5. Amount of snow transported determined by:
   a. Direction/velocity of wind;
   b. Area of 'fetch' (area from which snow is transported);
   c. Type of grain: loose, dry (old/new falling) is transported more easily over greater distance than wet, heavy snow. Yet drag sheer = heat, and spring winds (Chinooks/Foehns) can really accelerate MF Met.

B. **Barometric Pressure**
   1. Vapor pressure movement in snow is facilitated by lower Bp., and dry air of higher elevations.
   2. Change in atmospheric pressure = change in snowpack: an increase of 1 mb. = additional load of 10 cm. of 7% snow

C. **Humidity**
(% amount of H_2O vapor air is holding)
(% maximum it could hold at that temp.)
   1. Controls how far snow can be transported before it passes directly from solid to vapor, (sublimation).
   2. Relatively high humidity = greater snow transport. (Dry air sublimates so fetch may never reach loading zone.)
   3. Substantial increase/decrease of barometric pressure can trigger a pack release.
   4. Rain can only add heat and water.

Avalanche Terrain Identification

1. Slope Angles: 30°–40° primary hazard, 50°-60° in Andes; wet slush can slide at 15°.
2. Slide Paths: "Starting zone," "track" and "run-out zone."
   a. Starting zone: must be greater than 30° (see wet slush exception above); must be heavily loaded.
   - gullies and bowls are major collectors. "Most active starting zones are gullies bounded at the top by horseshoe ridges or cliffs." (p. 76, **Avalanche Handbook**)
   - starting zones are generally treeless, although slides may occur in heavily timber-

ed areas.
b. Track: may exist on slopes of at least 15°, generally 20° - 25° angles.
- tracks are channeled and unchanneled (i.e., gullies and chutes, or bowls, and headwalls) and may have multi-branched feeder tracks that empty into main track. Failure of snow on a feeder track may trigger release of main path
- depending on the size and density of a slide it can create new paths -- jumping gullies, breaking out at curves, clearing out new timber. Also, normal runout zones may become extended tracks, since some slides travel far beyond their normal reach and can continue uphill for great distances.
c. Runout zone RZ): debris of slide is 2 to 3-times denser snow than previous to its deposition and is much harder; wet slab debris can be almost ice-like. Huge cement-like blocks of corn and incredibly powerful clouds of loose, powder snow can cause damage and spread shattered trunks and tree limbs much farther than actual runout zones may suggest.

Route Finding in Avalanche Terrain
by Dale G. Gallagher

Prior to the Trip

Adequate planning and review will help make the trip successful. Weather data should be gathered -- past, present, and predicted. Several sources are usually available, such as National Weather Service Offices, radio and TV stations, newspapers, and the local Snow Ranger. Pay particular attention to long-range forecasts.

The factors that contribute to avalanches should be reviewed, such as wind, new snow, old snow, temperatures, and settlement. These should be analyzed against the past and present weather and snow conditions. Keep in mind that avalanche hazard varies from one climatic zone to another.

Routefinding/
Greg Dalbey
Photo

During the Trip

Throughout your trip, you need to be observant. Look at the terrain, the snow, and the weather.

Slide paths may be obvious, such as swathes through timber, gullies, or open slopes. However, scattered timber or small openings can also be avalanche areas. Short avalanches are killers -- 42% of the fatalities occur in slides that run less than 300 feet.

Consider the conditions of the old and new snow. How deep is the old snow and what was its surfcae? How deep is the new snow, what kind is it and what has it been doing? Is it slowly settling or does it have cracks over the surface? Look for avalanches that have run naturally. Note the direction this slope faces and the kind of avalanche it was.

Watch how the snow reacts under skis or snowshoes or snowmobiles. Do you see localized breaking of the snow surface or running cracks? Running cracks indicate the snow is tending to form slabs.

Has the wind been drifting the snow since the last storm? If so, try to analyze which slopes have been loaded.

And, during your trip, watch for even the slightest weather changes -- temperature, wind, clouds, etc., can indicate changes that may affect your trip.

Safe Time to Travel

The safe time to travel will vary.

During early and mid-winter, rapid temperature changes occur early morning and late afternoon. Travel is best during mid-day. However, in late winter, the mid-day and afternoon melting provides lubrication, which increases hazard. Travel should be done early or late in the day.

If a storm sets in, travel should be during the first few hours, or bivouac should be made until the hazard has abated. The highest danger exists during the storm and immediately afterwards. If cold temperatures are persistent, high hazard may exist for several days. Even in summer, at higher elevations, prolonged snowstorms may result in avalanche hazard.

Best Routes

Avoid known avalanche paths. If it is **necessary** to travel when there is suspected hazard, it is advisable to:

1. Stay on the windward side of ridges. If available, exposed rocks or wind scalloped snow are the safest routes.
2. In a "U" shaped valley, stay as far away from slopes with avalanche potential as possible.
3. In a narrow or "V" shaped valley, stay high on the slope, as close to fracture (crown) zone as possible.
4. Stay in **dense** timber. Avalanches **do** run through scattered timber.
5. Stay on rocky ridges that parallel avalanche paths, providing they protrude above the snow surface enough to avoid the snow sliding on either side of them. Know the terrain, since there may be additional avalanche paths above these ridges that will inundate them.
6. Stay off cornices. The view may be great,

but you may also experience a sudden "let down" feeling. Cornices may fracture in two different areas.

A primary fracture breaks near the lip and is usually a result of the buildup from the last storm. Secondary fractures occur further from the lip and are caused when the mass (weight) of an entire cornice exceeds the snow strength. Failure may occur at once, or a rupture crack (like a small crevasse) may develop and gradually widen over several days or weeks until the failure occurs. The crack may be hidden by a thin snow bridge.

7. Stay to the downhill side of crevasses on a glacier. A small avalanche can sweep a person into a crevasse and bury him deeply.

If you find it necessary to traverse the accumulation zone of an avalanche slope, take these precautions:

1. Ask yourself: Is it likely to slide?
   a. Will it probably slide?
   b. What will happen if someone does release it?
   c. What will we do then?
2. Remove or loosen equipment, such as ski pole straps, packsacks, buckles, etc.
3. Expose only **one** person at a time to danger. Others in the party should watch him to establish a "last seen" point if he is caught.
4. Stay as high as possible -- the closer you are to the fracture line (crown) the better chance you have to survive if the avalanche releases with you.
5. Use an avalanche cord, or better yet, an electronic signal sender such as the SKADI.
6. Use natural protection in your route. Rock outcrops, tree clumps, and other "islands" in the snow offer some protection.

7. **DO NOT** assume a slope is safe if it doesn't slide after the first man has crossed it. The accident reports prove that an avalanche can release after several people have already safely crossed it.

Remember, avalanche paths are the most dangerous routes and should be used only if there is no other feasible route.

In Summary

-- Know the weather
-- Know what causes avalanche hazard
-- Be properly equipped
-- Be observant
-- If you must travel in avalanche areas, choose your route very carefully
-- And, remember...
   1. Most people caught in avalanches started the slide themselves.
   2. Small avalanches kill 42% of the victims.

There is no magic formula...
-- Take time to think
-- Use good judgment
-- If your sixth sense says **no**, then don't **go**.

TOOLS FOR THE TELEMARKER

Climbing Skins, 'The Black Wax'

Carl Shumway -- who, with Dartmouth College friends, Fred Harris and J.Y. Cheney, made the first ski ascent of Mt. Washington on March 10, 1913 -- recalls scaling Mt. Moosilauke that same year: "Soon the climbing became so steep that we had to wind straps around our ski to keep from slipping backward." As in all things, 'necessity is the mother of ski-invention.'

Shumway's rediscovery of the age-old climbing skin was not to become popular in the U.S. for another fifty years, but today 'skins' are one of the most important tools in the ski-mountaineer's bag of tricks.

Once made from seal's skin, modern types consist of synthetic straps with a fur-like covering of fibre hairs on the outer side and which attach to the bottom of the skis from tips to tails. Because the hairs all lie in the same direction -- free ends angled to the tail -- they allow the ski to slide forward with relative ease, but catch in the snow and prevent the ski from slipping backward against their grain.

Very simple and very effective, climbing skins are the skier's equivalent of automotive 'posi-traction.' The first time I was the only skier in a party who didn't have skins was the last. After touring through eight miles of deep powder to reach the base of our intended slope, and facing a 1500' climb and descent before returning home the same day, I watched in amazement as my companions strapped-on and headed-up. Wax as I may and grunt as I might, I took a good fifteen minutes longer and covered twice the distance as they before reaching the top. When I got there, my arms were exhausted from the effort of holding my tenuous grip between ski and snow with the aid of my poles and the strength of my upper body.

We all had the same fine lines in our descent, but when we got to the bottom, the others skinned-up and skied another half-run before we all started back down-valley.

Since then, I never leave home without my climbing skins.

Their holding power on an incline is superior to that of waxes in almost all snow conditions, and enables a much more direct line of ascent. Instead of criss-crossing the middle of an un-tracked slope in a moderate uphill traverse, you can go almost right up the edge of the run, or better yet, through the trees that border it.

With skins' incredible grip you can follow not only the safest and fastest route, but the least strenuous as well. They do all the work; your upper body rests completely, and you can almost walk straight up with your hands in your pockets. They also enable you to wax primarily for the downhill run and virtually eliminate the need for klisters or continual scrapping of goey spring waxes.

Understanding the technical aspects of the snowpack, the mountain terrain and its weather, you are now in a position to understand what each of these things is telling you out there and what they mean to your security and skiing enjoyment.

Grab yourself a heavy-duty shovel. Find a relatively unexposed patch of snow, somewhere out of the wind and major sun, and start digging. Don't stop until you hit solid earth, no matter how deep it is. Plane-off the shaded face of your hole, making this wall as smooth as possible with the blade of your shovel. Stamp out a good space at the ground so you can work.

You now have a **snowpit**, and the history of the snowpack is written in the exposed layers of the pit wall before you.

Snow Pit Analysis

1. Procedure

 a. With a stiff card, go down through the snowpack, starting at the top of the pit wall and gradually working through each layer to the bottom. The relative pressures encountered will identify the individual layers and their textures and densities. Mark them off to the side with horizontal lines, or with toothpicks, etc.

 b. Slip your thermometer into the bottom-most layer that will support it. If an advanced TG layer or depth hoar exists at the ground (or bed) surface, which is usually the case in a mid-winter Rocky Mountain pack, you probably don't need to measure temp. here, or won't be able to because of the cohesionlessness of the grains.

 c. Draw a "snow profile" of the pit in your notebook, marking time of day, date, slope aspect, elevation, general weather (especially air temperature) at the top, measuring the total snowdepth with your pole, and then the same for the individual layers, recorded in an illustration of the horizontal profile of your pit wall.

 d. Move thermometer 10 cm. at a time up through layers and record. A 1°C temperature change (+) or (-) over a 10 cm. distance = a temperature gradient strong enough to cause weakening.

 e. Starting at the bottom, and using your cold scraper (or preferably a dark cold surface: eg. Parka sleeve), gather a few grain clusters from each identified layer and examine with hand lens. Note main grain types and their apparent trends, and the current state of their metamorphism (Beginning, Intermediate, Advanced). Measurement of grain size with side of Silva Compass and temperature gradients help you determine trends, as does density change.

 f. Assuming you are not a professional forecaster, helicopter guide, or incredibly interested and wealthy day tourer, you will not be in possession of the relatively costly scientific instrument known as a "RAM-PENETROMETER" and will therefore have to make a "rough" estimate of slab firmness. You are determining whether or not the slab is dense enough to carry the tension necessary for a slide. Obviously, fresh ET and advanced TG hoar layers are much less dense than ice, crusts, or wind slab

layers. A relative percentage equivalent of the densities may be determined as follows:
- If your gloved fist pressed perpendicular to the snow -- pit wall (applied gradually, and steadily), is all that is required to significantly deform the grains of any given layer inward (say, an inch or so), the slab is of low density, or described as 0% - 10% hardness (firmness).
- Four rigid fingers pressed perpendicularly = 10% to 20%.
- One finger = lower 20's - lower 30%.
- Pencil required to penetrate slab = 30 - 40%.
- Knife blade = 50%+; **very** hard.
- Very thin layers may best be recognized by their "feel" when cutting through them with your card. If stiff, hard resistance is met, a dense crust -- perhaps ice (rain, sleet), sun, or wind slab layer -- is indicated. If the layer is graupel, old surface-hoar TG, or thin ET, you card will "fall through" with little pressure -- as it will of course through the depth hoar TG at ground level. While they are easily overlooked because of their general thinness, the experienced "snow feeler" will keep a sharp eye and keen hand out for them. Whether of high or low density, they are 'weak' (or dangerous), layers. Loose, low density, cohesionless snow anywhere **within** the pack will collapse in a critical compression overload from heavier layers above, and hard crusts provide slick running (lubricating) surfaces in shear, tensile or compression failures. "Density measurements combined with snow grain type of layer provide a good idea of slab strengths." (P. Lev.) (Statistically, density profile alone gives a 60% meaningfulness; DP plus grain type gives 90% meaningfulness; [St. Lawrence]).

g. Shear strength of the bond between snow layers ("interfaces:" two parallel plane-surfaces in contact with one another), is adequately determined in two ways:
- With your shovel (after recording all your other information), cut away a segment of the pit wall in a 2-foot wide pillar, forming a 3-sided column of the snowpack. Place the blade of your vertically-held shovel into the back of the column from the top down, penetrating 2 layers or more, and then pull the shovel by the handle towards you with a light, quick jerk. The number of pulls (1 to 3 times) and the amount of force required to cause the bonds to fail and break away will give you a good idea of the strength of the various interfacing layers.
- Cut into the pack perpendicularly to the pit wall (as if you were making snow blocks for an igloo), and remove a cube that has a 2-layer interface running parallel to your shovel in its middle. Tilt your shovel to the approximate angle of the slope. From beneath, rap the shovel, lightly at first, with the palm of your hand. If one rap is all that is necessary to cause the top layer of the cube to shear away from the lower layer, the bond is said to be "tender" (weak, poor bonding). 2 raps = "moderate;" 3 = "tough."

h. After causing a shear failure, pick up slab layer (either one), turn over and examine the grain type existing at the now exposed interface with your hand lens. This will often reveal a lubricating layer (Ad. upper layer TG, graupel, old surface hoar, ice crust, etc.) that was otherwise missed.

The three prime factors of snowpack instability and high avalanche potential = presence of: a) sliding surface (crust, graupel); b) Dense slab (wind, wet, heavy); c) weak, collapsible layer; (Adv. TG, upper or ground level).

Add an increasing temperature trend, and look out!

Often these phenomena occur simultaneously within a given pack, creating the most unstable situation possible. Upper-level TG formation appears to be facilitated by the presence of a crust above or below; if weak TG develops below crust, a normally critical overload of new snow deposition will be temperarily supported by crust over collapsible layer.

If TG forms above crust (driven by crust itself) and is loaded with heavier snow, both a collapsible and sliding layer are present.

If your "gut feeling" apart from your analytical conclusion, tells you "danger ahead," pay attention to it. BE AWARE AND LIVE.

Examples of Likely Hazard Indicators

★ A lot of new snow (24"+ in 24 hours) or 1"/hour.
★ Heavy, wet new snow on weak, old snow (crust), or on top of lighter, new snow.
★ Heavy wind, continually increasing throughout storm.
★ Observed weak layer in pack.
★ Long, warm periods in spring.
★ Observed fracture lines, even small ones.
★ Settling (perhaps with fractures) indicated by audible "WHOOMPF!"
★ At height of major storm and for 24+/48(+) hours afterward.

Avalanche Rescue

Despite your intensive research into the avalanche phenomenon, your hazard forecast may still be incorrect, or conditions might change suddenly and dramatically. You may yet make some other mistake, or come upon a party which already has -- and immediate knowledge of avalanche-victim rescue is imperative.

The Rescue Plan Elements

1. Time
Keep foremost in mind the time-limit imposed upon human survival. Every minute counts in your plan. Every step must be accomplished in turn without omission in the fastest, safest manner possible.

2. Safety of Survivors
Friends have been buried, survivors and eye witnesses are distraught, frantic, and disoriented. KEEP YOUR WITS ABOUT YOU. HELP OTHERS GAIN COMPOSURE AS QUICKLY AS POSSIBLE BY YOUR CALM AND COMMANDING PRESENCE. **YOU** ARE RESCUE LEADER.

Your prime consideration is the safety of the

survivors. Although a slide has occurred, extreme hazard may still endanger your position.
* Analyze existing hazards
* Determine zone of safety
* (Determine) Line of retreat
* Move party **immediately** if you are in hazard area. You must stay alive even if it means delaying or calling off the rescue plan (no matter how emotionally abhorrent this may seem).
* Determine line of retreat from there.

3. The Eye Witness Account
* Calm survivors and/or eye witnesses
* Assure them of your competency, and
* Desire to rescue their friends quickly.

Obtain a rational account of the events leading up to, and during, the avalanche, such as:
* Number buried
* Avalanche protection in use? (Pieps or avalanche cords)
* Line of entry
* Last seen point
* Time elapsed since burial (may or may not be accurate)

4. Rescue Decision
Can a rescue be attempted in a reasonably safe manner for the survival of the living? It may indeed be a difficult situation to accept but this *must* remain the deciding factor.

5. Rescue Plan
* Formulate most likely location of person, persons from last seen spot (**mark**), location of surface objects (**mark**), path of slide, possible catch areas such as benches, trees, gully elbow, etc.
* Activate "**Avalanche Hazard Precautions**"

Avalanche Hazard Precautions for Searchers

* Turn pieps to receive and throw out your cords
* Be ready to turn your device to transmit upon signal from scout
* Undo all gear attachments: pack straps, pole straps, safety straps
* Wrap your mouth and eyes with scarf and goggles
* Be aware and ready to retreat to safety.
* **Post a lookout** in a zone of safety to warn rescuers of further threatening avalanche activity. Determine the means and nature of **warning signal**. Make sure all members know the signal and the path of retreat.
* Since time is of the essence and all rescue members are vital, **sending for help** may not be in order. Depending on the length of burial, size of avalanche, distance to help and number of total rescuers, you may want to make a preliminary search with all rescuers, sending for help after initial efforts are fruitless. This is generally made when a **survivor rescue plan becomes a body recover plan**. Even if you are only 15 minutes from help, a total elapsed time of 45 to 60 minutes for arrival of help is likely. People have been known to survive for quite awhile, however, and **additional rescue back-up** should be contacted at some point.
* MAKE A HASTY BUT THOROUGH SCUFF SEARCH. Start spreading out across slope at point of entry and work down. "Scuff" or scrape snow surface.
* Look for objects on, and just below, snow.
* Mark location of objects. Remember, a hand may lie just below a glove.

Avalanche Rescue Equipment

Stage 1
- Probes (3m./length)
- Heavy-duty shovels
- String line
- Flagging
- Emergency medical

Stage 2
- Revival and evacuation equipment
  -- Rescue transport
  -- Down bags
  -- Hot drinks
  -- Physician's kit/splints
  -- Resuscitation unit

★ Have your probe pole out and search with it around objects and likely areas of deposition as you work down swiftly

★ Line out rescuers at bottom of slide deposition with probe poles. Work up:

6. Standard Hasty Probe Search Line-Out
- Elbows on hips
- Rescuers elbow to elbow
- Probe in unison on command
- Raise probes to surface
- Advance 2 steps on command of leader.

7. Fine Probe: Body Recovery
- Fingertip-to-fingertip line-up
- 3 probes each: one at each foot and another in between. Number of probes = 13/m2
- Advance 30 cm.
- Overall probability = 100% with at least 1 strike likely (even in unfavorable body position)

8. Limited Manpower Over Large Area
- Leader uses cord (string line, rope, etc.) to keep line straight.
- The evenness of the level of probes at their top tells the rescue leader the location of a possible body
- The "feel" of an object tells the prober the nature of the object located
- A prober discovering a possible person should leave his probe in the location. The line should then advance, closing ranks around prober left behind, who should begin shoveling.
- Probe line continues.

TOOLS FOR THE TELEMARKER

Avalanche Essentials

Standard equipment for the ski-mountaineer, these items should be carried by all backcountry tourers who come anywhere **near** avalanche terrain at any time:

1. Avalanche rescue beacon: commonly known as a 'beeper,' this device emits and receives an electronic signal which enables fast, pinpoint location by rescuers skilled in its use of the burial victim who also wears one.

• Currently marketed under the trade names *Pieps®*, *Skadi®*, and *Echo®*, these units have replaced the avalanche cord as the most effective recovery system available, and are more than worth their additional expense or weight.

• Remember: no devise should be considered as *protection* from avalanche burial, or as a *guarantee* of survival. Likewise, a beeper is useless without another unit in the hands of someone who knows exactly what to do with it.

• Practice the procedures of beeper recovery on a regular basis. Make a contest of it: one person with a beeper takes a turn at locating a unit the other has buried in the backyard snow. Fastest time wins; everyone gets faster in the process and no one is ever fast enough.

2. Snow shovel: a tool of many uses, including camp-building, snowpit analysis and rescue work. A beeper without a shovel is as useless as a waterwell without a bucket: you have to be able to reach what it is you want once you've found it. Nothing works as well as a good shovel for digging out a buried friend.

• Size and weight should be secondary to the shovel's capacity to move snow effectively; one with a 'grain-scoop' shaped blade for dry snow, a good cutting edge for wet or icy slabs, rugged stem and powergrip handle works very well for most purposes.

3. Probe pole: an optional item of somewhat limited value for the recreational skier, the probe is nonetheless a mainstay for guides and rescue teams, and has saved many lives the world over. The standard models are composed of short segments of metal tubing which when screwed together measure 3-4 m. in length. Pointed at one end, the probe is driven down through the snow in search of a buried object: the difference between striking a person as opposed to striking, say, a boulder, is easily felt.

• Chances of finding an avalanche victim by

a thorough probe search are nearly 100%, but it is a slow process which is usually undertaken only when all other methods of recovery have failed.

• An excellent version of the basic design is marketed as a pair of ski poles which convert to form a single unit. By removing handles and baskets and joining the two ski pole shafts end-to-end, you have an effective probe, ready whenever you need it.

4. Snowpit analysis aids: the serious student of avalanche mechanics and snow stability will want to carry a few other special tools useful in field evaluation, such as:
• Hand-held magnifying lens (10x power);
• Waterproof notepad and reliable pen;
• Snow thermometer of the stem-and-face type;
• Stiff card (eg., metal scraper or mirror);
• Snow crystal identification chart.

Sustenance in a Can

Although I've never needed it, yet, the little, self-contained survival can is something I always take along on a ski trip, no matter what kind of belt pack or rucksack I might wear. Duct tape this thing to your leg if you have to, but wear something very much like it at all times.

The Rocky Mtn. Division of the PSIA/Nordic Instructors of America recommends in its 1978 **Ski Touring Instructor's Manual**, that this kit consists of a:

Metal can with sealing lid for boiling water, in which is included:

- candles
- plenty of waterproof matches
- salt and sugar tabs
- boullion cubes/instant protein mix
- tea and/or hot chocolate drink mix
- emergency space blanket
- good tape
- tools and extra ski/binding parts
- other goodies as will fit. (A metal pot-holder is nice.)

A container with dimensions similar to those of a 12 oz. *(net wt. 340g)*, zip-top, metal peanut can, for example, with an unmeltable lid will hold everything you need for an overnight emergency.

Recommended Reading for the Backcountry Skier:

Freedom of the Hills, (ed.) by Peggy Ferber (Seattle: the Mountaineers, 1974).

Medicine for Mountaineering, (ed.) by James A. Wilkerson (Seattle: The Mountaineers, 1967).

Backcountry Skiing, by Lito Tejada-Flores (San Francisco: Sierra Club Books, 1981).

Avalanche Handbook, by Ronald Perla and M. Martinelli, Jr. (Fort Collins: USDA Forest Service, Agriculture Handbook #489, 1976).

Snowy Torrents: Avalanche Accidents in the United States 1967-71, by Knox Williams (Fort Collins: USDA Forest Service, 1975).

Be An Expert with Map and Compass, Bjorn Kjellstrom (New York: Charles Scribner's Sons, 1967).

Winter First Aid Manual, NSPS, Inc.

Backcountry, Calvin Rustrum (Pittsboro: ICS Books) [#ICS 6215-PB]

The ABC's of Avalanche Safety, Dr. Edward La Chapelle.

Avalanches and Snow Safety, Colin Fraser.

Search and Rescue Dog Training, Sandy Bryson.

Looking for hidden treasure in the Dragon's Lair: Orizaba's volcanic rim/*M. Carr Photo*

VII EXPEDITIONS TO THE ULTIMATE EXTREME CROSS-COUNTRY

Something hidden, go and find it.
Go and look behind the Ranges
--something lost behind the Ranges.
Lost and waiting for you. Go!

Rudyard Kipling, The Explorer

The Meaning of 'Ski to Die'

"Pushing one's limits is a serious and potentially lethal game, to be approached intelligently, deliberately, with all possible caution and self-knowledge. Exalting a kamikaze attitude is childish and irresponsible."

John Borstelmann, Alta, WY.

"To push your limits, you must first know what your limitations are."

B.N. English, C.B., Co.

"There was no choice of routes, 'forward' being the only word...'Death or the west coast of Greenland'

Nansen

The expression, 'Ski to Die' has become a standard credo for telemarkers around the world -- one that symbolizes the spirit of the individual who accomplishes what has never been done before. It is the defiant response to those who cry, "It can't be done on skinny skis!" because no one else has even tried.

Yet, little skill is required to descend a slope like, 'The Man Who Fell Down Everest,' and any fool can commit suicide. 'Ski to Die,' then, is just an expression, meant to be taken only so far in practice. The intelligent skier -- nordic or alpine -- will not intentionally place himself in a situation where death is likely, yet must always realize death as a possibility that demands consideration. Thus, the object of extreme skiing (or any skiing), becomes a matter of survival

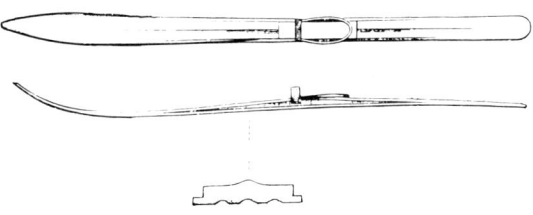

Nansen's telemark ski design

Fridtjof Nansen

with style.

Only by fully understanding the extent of his/her capabilities within the nature of opposing forces can the skier clearly analyze the available options, weight the odds, make a rational decision, proceed with confidence and act with absolute determination. Only then can anyone feel they have truly conquered, or even understood what it is that needs to be overcome.

One of the most daring expeditions ever undertaken, and perhaps the greatest ever accomplished on skis, was the first crossing of Greenland by Fridtjof Nansen and companions in 1888.

No one, until then, had been able to penetrate Greenland's arctic interior, and all attempts to even reach its eastern coast by ship had failed. Nansen had tried for a landing there in 1882, but his vessel was beset by outer ice, helplessly trapped for three weeks in the drifting floes off the rocky shore.

Realizing it was impossible to force a ship through such an awesome barrier, Nansen decided the only chance of crossing Greenland was by gaining land on foot and proceeding on ski. His plan was to make his way as far as possible aboard a Norwegian sealer, leave the vessel behind and travel over the ice pack to shore. From there, he was convinced a team could reach the west on ski, and succeed in exploring an unknown world on the crossing.

"In this way," wrote Nansen in his remarkable account, **The First Crossing of Greenland**, "one would burn all one's ships behind one (and) there would be no need to urge one's men on, as the east coast would at-

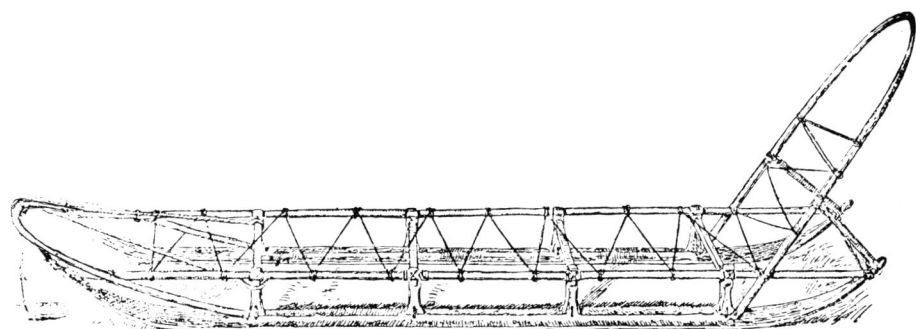

Nansen's sledge.

tract no one back...There was no choice of routes, 'forward' being the only word. The order would be: 'Death or the west coast of Greenland.'"

Nansen's desperate scheme relied heavily on ski mobility, and "all...prospects of success were based upon the superiority of 'ski' in comparison with any other means of locomotion..." He chose as his teammates three Norwegians and two Lapps who, like himself, were experienced 'ski-lobers' (from *lobe*: "to run"). Estimating such a party could cover 15-20 miles per day, Nansen calculated that the crossing would take no more than a month. They carried enough provisions for two months. In fact, their journey lasted five.

They took nine pair of skis, of Nansen's own design, specifically suited, he thought, to the conditions they would encounter in Greenland. Two pair were made of oak, 7'6½" long, with a sidecut that tapered from 3 5/8" wide at the shovel to 3 1/8" under the foot. The rest were of birch, narrower at the tip and without sidecut. The first type were made to turn, the second to go straight. They also carried 'trugers,' or Norwegian snowshoes, which were thought to be best suited to wet, sticky snow.

Their provisions were hauled behind them on sledges, also built to Nansen's innovative specifications. Unlike the large, heavy and narrow models then commonly in use, Nansen's sledges were strong, light and slender. The frames were constructed of ash, lashed together without pegs for greater elasticity. The runners were broader than most to run high in deep snow, and were made of elm or maplewood to glide easily on all kinds of surfaces. They were turned up both fore-and-aft, so the sledges could be dragged equally well from either end.

The remainder of their gear was selected with similar attention, and the team was as thoroughly equipped as possible to meet the potential extremes of the inland ice. Their technical skills were just as sophisticated, and each member was as capable as he was courageous.

Roald Amundsen's Antarctic team

Before setting sail from Christiania, Norway on May 2nd, the members of the 1888 Greenland Expedition took a skiing lesson from the pros in Telemark. Says Nansen: "(They) showed us that when one has really learned to control one's ski without having continuous recourse to one's staff (like a witch's broomstick), one obtains a mastery over them which is quite impossible in the other case."

Yet the conditions they encountered on their journey were so miserable that neither equipment nor technique could master them. They found the snow "fine as dust," packed by the wind into drifts "on which ordinary ski will scarcely move at all...this was the kind of snow we had to deal with during nearly the whole of our crossing of the inland ice, and was the reason why our progress was so very slow and wearisome."

"Had we come earlier in the season, we should have found an excellent, hard and slippery surface...and the crossing would not have taken us so long." In spite of their bad timing and the difficulties they encountered before finally reaching the west coast of Greenland on September 29th, their ultimate success was due mainly to their skis. "Without their help," maintained Nansen, "we should have advanced a very little way, and even then died miserably or have been compelled to return."

Britain's Sir Ernest Shackleton was another famous explorer who used skis on several expeditions into the unknown. He had twice tried to be the first person to reach the South Pole, and in 1909 had gotten to within 97 miles of his goal before being forced to turn back. Despite his efforts, Roald Amundsen eventually claimed the South Pole for Norway in 1912, reaching it on skis.

Yet Shackleton was determined to conquer Antarctica as no known human had ever done before him, and in 1915 his Imperial Trans-Antarctica Expedition set sail, its course bound for the bottom of the world. The expedition's goal: to cross the southernmost continent overland by ski from east to west.

Although Shackleton and his men failed to ever reach the coast of Antarctica, and their skis were of little use on the shifting ice-floes of the Weddell Sea, their 497-day-long ordeal was a remarkable feat of endurance; and their eventual survival to the man against incredible odds is an inspiration for all explorers ever after.

When compared to the adventures of Nansen, Shackleton and other great explorers of skiing history, the 1980 "Green Duck" Expedition to Labrador by Steve Monfredo, Peter Dea and Andy Lapkas (members of the CB "Ski to Die Club") might seem a modest endeavor. Yet on this trip into Labrador's arctic ranges, three young cross-country skiers telemark-turned down peaks unskied since prehistoric times and traveled for 33 days through remote wilderness, totally cut off from civilization and the possibility of rescue. Relying on individual skill and courage, confident in the strength of their team and the extensive preparations behind their plan, these three accomplished a dream and in the process discovered a part of what backcountry skiing is all about. In this sense, their journey was equal to any ever undertaken, and their experiences just as profound.

From the excerpts by Peter Dea and others that follow, I think you'll understand something of the challenges involved in any extended expedition of this sort. Also, you'll get an idea of the rewards that await "out there," and of the ultimate joy to be found by exploring new horizons of nature and self on cross-country skis.

Dr. Cook on skis

Sledging in the Arctic Circle/ *Peter Dea Photo*

March 31, 1980

The Arctic barrens surrounding us are a desolate sight. Mile after mile we see only a landscape of rolling hills smoothed and rounded by the Laurentide ice-sheet long ago, pitted by elongated lakes of all sizes now frozen between the rocky hills.

Ahead lies our route: up the Koroc River to the Palmer Divide, then into the Torngat Mountains. After telemark skiing a huge, unnamed peak, we will return by way of the Koroc to George River again. May God be with us as the unexpected is before us...

Raw, desolate, brusque, wild, white, black, rough...why would anyone want to venture through land which evokes such stark impressions? Remembering the shining eyes of our Eskimo driver, who had shuttled our gear on his snowmobile to the trailhead, I sensed an answer.

His deep-cleft wrinkles, etched in bold relief upon his smiling countenance, hinted at the wealth of wisdom and sagacity gained by his people over countless generations. His high cheekbones and flattened forehead, framed by a halo of fur, testified to both an inherent strength forged by a continuing conflict with the elements, and an enduring respect for life steeped in centuries of tradition and experience.

Here, I thought, was my reason: what I really sought was an understanding of how this staunch face and proud soul were created, how his expressive rivers of knowledge were formed, and how his love for the land, his people, his past and future were gained. His spirit was to accompany us every mile as we skied

Nansen's caravan across Greenland

deeper into this remote, almost mystical arctic realm, searching in the roots of his existence a reason for our own.

April 2, 1980

Slide right, slide left, one ski past the other, step after step...constantly nagged by the sleds and 500 pounds of gear we haul behind. It's bad enough pulling the damn things on the level -- just like tugging a Winnebago -- but skiing into the smallest bump is really annoying. First a tug from the rear as the sled hangs back, a slight push as she eases off the crest, then watch out for that buck as you hit the flats.

Often there is sand frozen into the crusty snow, and the sled stops dead in its tracks. If badly loaded, or turned the wrong way, over she goes. It's rough but really better than carrying 150 pounds on your back.

September 11, 1887

...Balto stopped and said to me: "When you asked us two Lapps in Christiania how much we could pull we said that we could manage a hundred-weight. But now we have two hundred-weight apiece, and all I can say is that if we drag these loads across to the west coast we are stronger than horses.'
Nansen, **First Crossing of Greenland**

"However hard the day had been, however exhausted we were, and however deadly the cold, all was forgotten as we sat around our cooker, gazing at the faint rays of light which shone from the lamp and waiting patiently for our supper. Indeed I do not know many hours in my life on which I look back with greater pleasure than these."
Nansen, **First Crossing**

*"It happened not infrequently that when we took our shoes off at night, they, our thick socks and ordinary stockings were all frozen together into a solid mass...On these days the temperature of the air at noon rose to between -4° Fahr. (-20° Cent.), and 5° Fahr. (-15° Cent.). This was the middle of September, and these temperatures are without any comparison the lowest that have **ever been recorded at the time of year** anywhere on the face of the globe."*
Nansen, **First Crossing**

"The whole heaven blazed, both north and south; the lights swept onward, and then returned again; and suddenly a whirlwind swept to pass across the sky, driving flames before it, and gathering them together at the zenith, where there was a sparkling and a crackling as of a burning fire, which almost dazzled the eyes of the onlooker."
Nansen, **First Crossing**

A warm fire sure feels comforting after a long day in the traces: a refuge to look forward to and a source of renewal. Its grace is an integral part of fellowship in the midst of an inhospitable wilderness, breathing warmth and assurance back into the human spirit. Here we share the memories of past adventures and plan future dreams.

April 4, 1980 -- Beach Ramp Camp

Frigid, windy. Nine miles.

Each day's temperature is gauged by the ice in our boots. Today, a layer 1/8" thick has accumulated between our inner liners and outer shoe. It took a good hour to melt it out by the fire -- that's scary!

The howling wind is brutal.

In the evening, calmness reveals a brilliant menagerie of stars and planets, now partially masked by the streaming clouds of Aurora Borealis.

The sky is filled with the lime-hued glow of the Northern Lights...a point source eminating from the headwaters of the Koroc and blossoming westward over our camp. Parts of this radiating flower-pattern would disband, sending streamers outward in broad curls that wrapped themselves northward. As they uprooted their trunks and vanished, others would appear.

Although stationary for several minutes, this vast arc began to move rapidly as if someone had suddenly whipped the end of a blanket, sending ripples down its length. As the waves stacked up in the east, the intensity of their brilliance grew, until finally the last ripple followed the dimming procession to total extinc-

April 6, 1980

Much of the river ice had been swept clean of snow, exposing its slick blue surface to our skis. Wax didn't matter a bit today since the strong westerly wind literally blew us upstream. I was awed at how fast and with what ease we sailed along with 150 pounds of gear behind us. Just pick up your poles, lift your arms and off you flew with record speed...sometimes too fast for comfort. I worried about getting blown into an open lead in the ice: splash, freeze, all worries extinct.

Turning into the wind for more than a few moments meant risking frostbite, and this is no place to lose a nose. Here Nature draws a thin line between life and death.

April 7, 1980

The full day of horrid storm took its toll on our minds and bodies, demanding a partial day of rest. There is only so much one can stand out here and we had been pushed to our limits. Yet an intangible inner force drives me, encouraging my soul when my heart says, "No!," flowing outward to push me on. Arrgghh...Persevere!

"Sailing on the Inland ice"

Icefall in Labrador/P. Dea Photo

The force and severity of the evening's wind were well inscribed in the snow for us to decipher. An intricately constructed sculpture of small drifts -- or "Sastrugie" -- had formed where our tracks had been less than 20 hours before, and a large cornice we had broken off was completely rebuilt -- overnight!

On the first part of the trip we had worried about the river breaking up early and stranding us far upstream. Now, the thought of skiing into this wind on our return chilled us even more. Could we make it back safely...if delayed, would we have enough food? Should we turn back now, or go on?

None of us have the answers to these questions. Decisions can be so hard when our lives and well being of our families is at stake.

We agreed to ski to the last patch of trees tomorrow. There, we will feel out the weather, our gut feelings, physical and mental strengths, and make our decision.

April 10, 1980 -- Day 11

Awake. It's quiet, still, outside -- strange change; golden light filters through our tent roof. I poke my head out. A beautiful, deep blue sky greets my stormy eyes. I yell out a "YAHOO!" The weather heralds the go-ahead for the Torngats! There's no stopping now!

Slowly the curtain of mist draws back and we have a clear view directly up the wide, flat Koroc River. All looks so graceful: virgin snowfields and rounded banks funnel our vision to the majestic sight ahead. With eyes glued to the peaks, we ski on.

We pass numerous tracks running all over the hills, and soon spot a herd of 30 caribou. Their coats are lighter than any I have ever seen, making them almost indistinct against the white hillside. Soon we are surrounded by many small herds. They seem to be everywhere. Incredibly, one herd ran down the mountain, and headed straight for Fredo and I. On they charged, their hoofbeats thundering across the wind-crusted snow, until, just 100 feet from where we stood, they veered off and trotted east.

Then, coming over a knob one hundred meters away, a jet black arctic wolf appears. He stopped, looked inquisitively around, then leapt a cornice (airtime), and scampered up the river. Where there's caribou, there roam wolves. The presence of each adds so much to the feeling of the wilds, especially when they are running right in front of you.

From the Koroc to the broad mellow pass ahead we slowly climbed towards Labrador. Rising over the last knoll, the entire relief of the mountains aligning the Palmer drops our jaws.

After absorbing all this in a few moments, we embraced each other, for we had finally made it to Labrador. Such a strenuous journey it had been, but thoughts of all the pain and misery faded as we stood in awe at the pass.

What a fine feeling to expose yourself to this awesome land, so remote from society. It's a free feeling that expands my mind, and allows me to look beyond normal life patterns, into a truer sense and existence where Mother Nature reigns supreme, where harmony exists between all. Here, a day of sunshine balances a week of storm. Such a trip, and the experiences of a few weeks in the wild, even balance my life back in town. Some parts will stick with me a lifetime.

April 11, 1980 -- Torngats/Palmer Divide
Day 12

After a leisurely breakfast we began our ascent of the great mountain that had lured us on so long and far. Despite our fatigue, our enthusiasm carried us higher and higher. Finally, we were there, and all the Torngats lay before us.

The Descent

Then, we pinned on our narrow nordic skis and telemarked 4,000 vertical-feet over a five-mile stretch of mountain...definitely a Big Mountain whatever we name it!

Once down to the first saddle we dismounted and walked across the rocks, then found some nice open western exposures to ski which dropped us out into the meadow below.

I have never skied with such an awesome view: between turns you could glance out and see for 40 miles -- all barren, all wild. We're thankful to Ma Nature for such a splendid day -- one of the most memorable of my life.

"China Dune", by Bob Jamieson

PLACE: Atop a thousand foot sand dune, in a valley rimmed by 24,000 foot peaks. Below, the valley of Ekke-bel-su. Part of the land called Xingiang. The roof of the world. Somewhere here is the mythical city of Janaider, perhaps buried beneath these very dunes. The mountains are the Pamirs...variously claimed by Russia, China, Pakistan, Afghanistan and India. Ice and rock, alpine desert. And sand...

TIME: September, 1982. A giant step back in

Steve Monfredo in Labrador/P. Dea Photo

time for six young Canadians, back into a land and people unchanged since the passing of Marco Polo. A pastoral land of yaks and tough little horses and fat-tailed sheep, a land uncluttered by the world of commerce since the silk trade expired a few centuries ago...

To this time and place we came, six foreigners, four climbers and two wives, for a practice ascent of Muz-Tagh-Ata, a technically simple but anatomically harsh climb of 24,757-feet, in preparation for an attempt on Evertest in the fall of 1982. The climb, accomplished without major problems (an easy way to write off a jillion calories), included skiing from the summit and setting a world altitude record for the telemark turn.

Afterwards, while sitting in the base camp, three of us -- Pat Morrow, Lloyd Gallagher and Dr. Steven Bezruchka -- decided to try some even more esoteric skiing...Dune skiing!

A wind full of harsh sand, in a land harsh and hard and lonely beyond all telling. We have no speed, and thus, no momentum. Utter balance is required, subtle concentration in the ball of the foot. Floating down through a dreamscape...the thin hiss of my edges is lost in the howl of the wind, our turns lengthen as the slope decreases. At the edge of the dunes we slide out into the grass...!! *Reprinted with permission from* **Powder Magazine**

The 1982 Mt. Everest Grand Circle Expedition
by Ned Gillette

The days are long gone where there are huge voids on the map to be explored, or the highest peaks to be conquered for the first time. Today, the essence of adventuring is style. There is still plenty left to do -- you just have to use your imagination in a different way. For Reinhold Messner, the style is to climb 8,000 meter peaks with little support, expense or oxygen..[As of 1983, Reinhold's achievement of being the first known human to have reached the highest peak on the face of the earth in alpine style without the aid of containerized oxygen still holds.]

The idea of tackling Mt. Everest horizontally instead of vertically came to me while staring at a map...spread out on the floor. Everest! Of course. The ultimate lodestone. The third pole...Why not look at an old subject in a new way? Our goal suddenly grew to be the first climbers and skiers to go completely around the highest mountain on earth...

Jan Reynolds and I were the two fortunate enough to make it all the way around. We brought others onto the team to strengthen it for different legs -- Jim Bridwell, Steve McKinney, Craig Calonica, and Rick Barker - but at no time were there more than four in the field. A small, self-sufficient team has become the hallmark of our expeditions.

On December 1st we arrived at Katmandu, Nepal, then flew to Lukla. A six-day trek through Sherpa country brought us to base camp under Mount Pumori at 17,500'. Pumori, which means "Daughter Peak" in Nepalese, stands on the Nepal/Tibet border, just west of Everest.

The month-long climb to its 23,442-foot summit was the beginning to our circumnavigation...We climbed a new route on the east ridge, thus becoming the first Americans to successfully climb in the Himalaya in the winter.

...We had to cross over three 20,000-foot passes, each as high as Mt. McKinley. No new snow had fallen in the past 50 days. The ice was bullet-proof. Our original plan to ski over the passes became impossible...

With that crossing accomplished, our first semi-circle was complete...After coming home for a rest, we were back at it in Tibet in mid-April...

Much of our route around the northern half of Everest would be in the footsteps of the 1921 British reconnaissance during their search for the most practical route up the Tibetian side. (But)...we were doing something on cross-country skis that nobody had ever done before -- ski in Tibet.

We climbed a beautiful 23,000-foot virgin peak and then skied for five days in the upper East Ronbuk Glacier at 21,000 feet...Next, we climbed over the 22,000-foot Lhakpa La and the 20,000-foot Karp La passes into the Kangshung Glacier Basin.

The circle was thus completed on May 16th...for us, one of the greatest mountain adventures imaginable.

excerpted from **Phoenix Newsletter**, 1982

"Three-pin Skiing the Andes: A First Descent,"
by David Blehert

After five warm-up peaks ranging from 18,000 to 19,500 feet, all first descents on any kind of skis, four members of our party decided to attempt Nevado Ausengate, the highest peak in the Cordillera Vilcanota in southern Peru.

Crampons are replaced by three-pin bindings; ice axes and hammers, by high tech avalanche probe ski poles, and we point our long, skinny boards down the mountain.

The first slope is steep and exposed and a fall would be fatal. Our euphoria must be guarded until we negotiate the initial narrow section with a bergschrund on the left and a 4,000 foot vertical drop on the right. A few quick turns, some freefall, a pole plant, a bit of a rush, like on the first drop of a rollercoaster after a long climb, and we are below the tip of the peak and ready for the endless run.

Telemark turn after turn, laughter, silence, swoosh of our skis on the perfectly white, sparkling, untouched snow.

Reprinted from **Lowe Alpine Systems 10th Anniversary Catalog** (© 1983)

Rick Wyatt's Nordic Descent of the Grand Teton, Wyoming
(Elev.: 13,770-feet; June 10, 1982)

Many people, including several close friends, have told him they consider an attempt to ski the Grand on nordic skis suicidal.

But this is not an impulse for Wyatt...He is pursuing a quest which requires what one writer called, "firm ideas about discipline and humility." Together these two qualities form a razor's edge upon which the mountaineer must balance. On the one hand, he must grasp fully where the true limitations lie, even when they are beyond what others think possible; on the other, he must have the humility to back down when the real risks become too great....

"I do not think any of it is worth getting hurt over, let alone getting killed...You don't want to be left with a feeling that you lucked out. You want to feel you could repeat the act safely, again and again...I like to expand my limitations, but with a considerable margin of error. If I were to ever view my chances as 50/50, I wouldn't consider the act.

But at the same time, I realize and prepare for the very real possibility that I might get pushed right out to the edge. It often happens in the mountains."

For a nordic skier the condition of the snow is of supreme importance; this is the cleaver, the dividing line, between what is possible on nordic gear versus downhill...

"In some ways nordic gear is an advantage in that if you are skiing well, staying in position, it seems to be clearer as to when you are approaching the point when the skis will no longer hold. On nordic gear there is simply a limit to what your ankle will support (and where the metal of the protruding binding will begin to catch and deflect the ski's edge."

A nordic ski descent of the Grand Teton is important, not only because it was a first, or even because Wyatt succeeded at all, but because like an ascent of Everest without oxygen, Wyatt's accomplishment places the emphasis not on the tools which man creates, but back on man himself. Wyatt purposely chose nordic gear over downhill because it made for a better adventure.

> Chris Noble, "The Grand Adventure,"
> **Powder Magazine**

Each of us has our own definition of ski adventure, our own method of approach and sense of style. At the same time, we all follow the same path, and our wanderings on it express a common urge to seek new horizons, to expand the boundaries of our world and thus our place within it. Along the way, we share a similar experience of freedom and joy, and in the end, come to know ourselves for the first time.

It is the unbridled mind of man, more than the limited nature of his tools, that makes such quintessential understanding possible.

To search for the old is to understand the new
　The old, the new
This is a matter of time.

In all things man must have a clear mind.

The Way:
　Who will pass it on straight and well?
> Gichin Funakoshi
> **The Master Text**

FOOTNOTES

Chapter II

[1] Ted Bays, **Nine Thousand Years of Ski: Norwegian Wood to French Plastic** (Ishpeming: Nat'l. Ski Hall of Fame Press, 1980), p. 1

[2] **Webster's 7th Collegiate Dictionary** (Springfield: G. & C. Merriam Co., Pub., 1971), p. 815

[3] Art Burrows, "The Telemark Comes Full Circle", **Ski X-C: The Cross Country Magazine** (New York: Ziff-Davis Pub. Co., Winter, 1983), p. 98

[4] Richard Needham (ed.), **Ski Magazine's Encyclopedia of Skiing** (New York: Harper & Row, Pub., Inc., 1970), p. 2

[5] Bays, **op. cit.**, p. 6

[6] Needham, **op. cit.**, p. 20

[7] Charles M. Dudley, **60 Centuries of Skiing** (Brattleboro: Stephan Day Press, 1935), p. 25

[8] **ibid.**, p. 19

[9] C. Brinton, J. Christopher & R. Wolff, **A History of Civilization** (New Jersey: Prentice-Hall, Vol. I, 1967), p. 12

[10] Dudley, **op. cit.**, p. 18

[11] Bays, **op. cit.**, p. 1

[12] **The Last Two Million Years: A Reader's Digest History of Man.**

[13] Needham, **loc. cit.**

[14] **ibid.**

[15] Dudley, **op. cit.**, p. 32

[16] **ibid.**, p. 33

[17] Bays, **op. cit.**, p. 21

[18] Dudley, **loc. cit.**

[19] Stein Eriksen, **Come Ski with Me** (New York: W. W. Norton & Co., 1966), p. 24

[20] **ibid.**, p. 20

[21] Dudley, **op. cit.**, p. 34

[22] **ibid.**, p. 33

[23] Eriksen, **op. cit.**, p. 17

[24] **ibid.**

[25] **ibid.**

[26] Dudley, **op. cit.**, p. 61

[27] Lowell Thomas, **Good Evening Everybody** (New York: W. Morrow & Co., Inc., 1976), p. 120

[28] William Stevenson, **A Man Called Intrepid** (N.Y.: Random House, 1976).

[29] Dudley, **op. cit.**, p. 64

[30] Fridtjof Nansen, **The First Crossing of Greenland** (London: Longmans, Green & Co., 1910), pp. 59-60

[31] Eriksen, **op. cit.**, p. 23

[32] **ibid.**

[33] Nansen, **op. cit.**, pp. 62-63

[34] Eriksen, **op. cit.**, p. 18

[35] Bays, **op. cit.**, p. 48

[36] **ibid.**, p. 67

[37] **ibid.**, p. 47

[38] Dudley, **op. cit.**, pp. 42-43

[39] Burrows, **loc. cit.**

[40] Robert W. Parker, **Ski and Snow** (T.J. Mahoney, 1960), pp. 73-78

[41] Eriksen, **op. cit.**, p. 21

[42] **ibid.**

[43] **ibid.**

[44] Bill Berry, **Ski Magazine**

[45] Eriksen, **loc. cit.**

[46] Dudley, **op. cit.**, pp. 46-47

[47] Parker, **loc. cit.**

[48] Eriksen, **loc. cit.**

[49] Parker, **loc. cit.**

[50] **ibid.**

[51] Dudley, **op. cit.**, pp. 44-45

[52] Parker, **loc. cit.**

[53] Duane Vandenbusche, **The Great Snowshoer of the Gunnison Country, Crested Butte Magazine,** winter, 1982.

[54] Dudley, **op. cit.**, p. 55

[55] **ibid.**,

[56] **ibid.**, p. 57

[57] **ibid.**

[58] **ibid.**

[59] Burrows, **loc. cit.**

REFERENCE FOOTNOTES, "CH. III: Telemark Turning Today..."

[1] J. Major and Olle Larrson, **World Cup Ski Technique** (Laporte: Poudre Publishing Co., 1979), p. 18

[2] Masatoshi Nakayama, **Dynamic Karate: Instruction by the Master** (Tokyo: Kodansha International LTD., 1966), p. 58

[3] Allan Barra, "The Lessons of Master Seo," **Esquire Magazine,** Aug. 1982; p. 22

[4] Gichin Funakoshi, **Karate-Do-Kyohan: The Master Text** (Tokyo: Kodansha International LTD., 1973), p. 40

[5] Major & Larrson, **loc. cit.**

[6] **ibid.**, pp. 111-112

REFERENCE FOOTNOTES: "Chapter IV: Sp. Conditions

[1] Paul Parker, "Nordic 'Pre-Turn Ideas' ", **Phoenix Newsletter,** Winter, 1983

[2] Wayne Hanson, "Cross-Country Downhill", **Cross-Country Skier Magazine,** Nov. 81, p. 34